JOSEPH CH
&
SAM SHEPARD

Letters and Texts,
1972–1984

JOSEPH CHAIKIN
&
SAM SHEPARD

Letters and Texts, 1972–1984

Edited by
Barry Daniels

THEATRE COMMUNICATIONS GROUP
1994

Joseph Chaikin & Sam Shepard: Letters and Texts, 1972–1984 is published by Theatre Communications Group, Inc., 355 Lexington Ave., New York, NY 10017.

Originally published by New American Library, a division of Penguin Books USA, Inc.

Chaikin, Joseph, 1935–
    Joseph Chaikin & Sam Shepard: letters and texts, 1972–1984 / edited by Barry
Daniels.
        ISBN 1-55936-095-X
        1. Shepard, Sam, 1943– —Correspondence. 2. Chaikin, Joseph, 1935–
—Correspondence. 3. Shepard, Sam, 1943– —Authorship—Collaboration. 4. Theatrical
producers and directors—United States—Correspondence. 5. Experimental theater—United States.
I. Shepard, Sam, 1943– . II. Daniels, Barry V. III. Title IV. Title: Joseph Chaikin and Sam Shepard.
[PS3569.H394Z486 1994]
812'.5409—dc20
[B]
                                                                            94-29134
                                                                                CIP

First TCG Edition, October 1994

You can make a fresh start with your final breath.

—Brecht

A C K N O W L E D G M E N T S

Auerbach, Doris. "Speaking in Tongues: Exploring the Inner Library." Reprinted with the permission of Twayne Publishers, an imprint of Macmillan Publishing, from *Sam Shepard, Arthur Kopit and the Off Broadway Theatre* by Doris Auerbach. Copyright ©1982 by G.K. Hall & Co.

Blumenthal, Eileen. "Sam Shepard and Joseph Chaikin: Speaking in Tongues." From *American Dreams: The Imagination of Sam Shepard*, edited by Bonnie Marranca. Copyright ©1980 by Eileen Blumenthal. This essay appeared in a slightly different form in the *Village Voice* and in the author's Cambridge University Press publication, *Joseph Chaikin: Exploring at the Boundaries of Theatre*. Reprinted with the permission of PAJ Publications and the author.

Everett-Green, Robert. "Chaikin Speaks in the Voice of an Angel." From *The Globe and Mail*, Toronto, June 13, 1986. Copyright © 1986 by *The Globe and Mail*. Reprinted with the permission of *The Globe and Mail* and the author.

Gussow, Mel. "Intimate Monologues That Speak to the Mind and Heart." From the *New York Times*. December 9, 1979. Copyright © 1979 by The New York Times Company. Reprinted by permission.

Kleb, William. "Shepard and Chaikin Speaking in Tongues." From *Theatre*, vol. 10, no. 1 (Fall 1978). Copyright © 1978 by William Kleb. Reprinted with the permission of *Theatre* and the author.

Leverett, James. "Other Voices." From the *Soho Weekly News*, November 22, 1979. Copyright © 1979 by James Leverett. Reprinted by permission.

Shepard, Sam and Chaikin, Joseph. "Tongues." Copyright © 1981 by Sam Shepard. "Savage/Love." Copyright © 1981 by Sam Shepard. From *Seven Plays* by Sam Shepard. Copyright © 1981 by Sam Shepard. Reprinted with the permission of Bantam Books, a division of Bantam

Contents

Preface

On May 7, 1984, Joseph Chaikin suffered a stroke during open-heart surgery. As the summer began, he started the difficult process of recovery. In addition to excellent medical therapy, Chaikin had the support of friends and family, who helped him regain the language he had lost and helped him continue his work as a director and performer. Sam Shepard's visit with Chaikin in August 1984 resulted in the creation of a monologue, "The War in Heaven," which was the first professional project Chaikin completed during the early stages of his recovery.

During that summer I was asked by Chaikin's friends if I thought any of the papers in Chaikin's archives, housed at Kent State University where I was teaching, might be worthy of publication. At the time, I felt there were several possible publications from the papers, but the one that clearly stood out as being both manageable and of general interest was a book bringing together the texts, letters, and other documents relating to the creation of "Tongues," "Savage/Love," and "The War in Heaven." Such a book would, I thought, offer a fascinating picture of both artists as well as provide insight into the process of collaboration in the theatre.

I am indebted to many kind and generous people for help in tracking down documents and assembling this book. The two most important sources of the papers used in this book are the Chaikin Archive in the Rare Books and Manuscripts Division, Department of Special Collections of the Kent State University Library and the Shepard Collection in the Department of Special Collections of the Mugar Memorial Library at Boston University. Alex Gildzen, Curator of Special Collections at Kent State, deserves special mention for his willingness to locate uncatalogued material and field numerous questions that came up in the editing process.

Howard B. Gotlieb, Curator of Special Collections at the Mugar Memorial Library, helped facilitate my research in Boston. I would also like to thank the staffs of the Performing Arts Collection of the New York Public Library at Lincoln Center and of the Archives of the New York Shakespeare Festival.

Thanks are also due to the authors who allowed me to reprint their reviews or essays: Doris Auerbach, Eileen Blumenthal, Robert Everett-Green, Mel Gussow, William Kleb, James Leverett, and Bernard Weiner. Sandra Eaglen provided invaluable assistance proofreading the manuscript. Eva Dorsey helped with the typing and offered valuable comments on the manuscript as I was completing it. The Office of Research and Sponsored Programs, Kent State University, provided funding during the period I was collecting the documents in this book.

Finally, of course, I want to thank Joseph Chaikin and Sam Shepard for making their papers available to me and cooperating throughout the process of assembling this book. Although it covers only a small part of their equally distinguished careers, it conveys a spirit that has remained constant in all their work: a passionate interest in the process of creating theatre and in exploring the poetic and musical qualities of language.

NOTE: Parts of the texts of the letters have been deleted for reasons of privacy and/or interest. Punctuation has been added for clarity and spelling has been corrected. Dates have often come from postmarks on the envelopes. Dates in brackets are conjectural.

-- 1 --

Chaikin and Shepard: Establishing a Dialogue

On the Lower East Side there was a special sort of culture developing. You were so close to the people who were going to the plays, there was really no difference between you and them—your own experience was their experience, so that you began to develop that consciousness of what was happening . . . I mean nobody knew what was happening, but there was a sense that something was going on. People were arriving from Texas and Arkansas in the middle of New York City, and a community was being established. It was a very exciting time.[1]

This community Shepard found when he arrived in Manhattan in 1963 had its theatrical voice in the off-off-Broadway theatre, a rich and vital movement which can be traced to the Living Theatre's 1959 production, at its new space on 14th Street, of Jack Gelber's *The Connection*. It has been described as presenting

> the audience with a kind of theatre it had not seen before. Its form was indigenous to their life-style and its language was completely contemporary. . . . The theatre was beginning to renew itself as ceremony and the audience was able to relate and participate; it could not deal with the play as if there were a fourth wall. The critics, who usually shape the public taste, were ignored. This was an audience theatre and the new audience was interested.[2]

The Living Theatre was at the center of the off-off-Broadway theatre movement until the IRS closed its theatre in October 1963, and the company began its European exile in 1964. By that date, off-off-Broadway theatre was flourishing in small cafés and workshop theatres. There seemed to be little money but limitless energy and enthusiasm. There was a definite interest in developing new American playwrights and exploring non-naturalistic modes of performance as well as in creating ensembles. In addition to the Living Theatre, which had been founded by Julian Beck and

[1]

Judith Malina in 1951, there was the Caffe Cino, started in 1959 by Joe Cino; the Judson Poets' Theatre, founded by Al Carmines and Lawrence Kornfeld in 1961; La Mama ETC, founded by Ellen Stewart in 1962; the Open Theatre, formed as a workshop in 1963; Theatre Genesis, founded by Ralph Cook in 1964; and Wynn Handeman's American Place Theatre, opened in 1964. In these theatres the work of a new generation of American playwrights was heard: Rosalyn Drexler, Terrence McNally, Jean-Claude van Itallie, Lanford Wilson, Rochelle Owens, Megan Terry, Marie Irene Fornés, Paul Foster, Adrienne Kennedy, and Sam Shepard. Ensemble creation was explored by the Living Theatre in its European pieces, *Mysteries, Frankenstein,* and *Paradise Now,* and by the Open Theatre, and later by the Performance Group, formed in 1968 by Richard Schechner.

The off-off-Broadway theatre of the 1960s existed in reaction to the mainstream, essentially realist theatre of Broadway and the increasing conservatism—and escalating costs—of off-Broadway, where experimentation had become largely a matter of producing plays from the European avant-garde. Middle-class values were generally questioned and/or ridiculed in the off-off-Broadway theatres of the 1960s. This was a period of social upheaval in the country, reflected in the protests against American involvement in the Vietnam War and in the civil rights movement. The alternative theatre was, then, often a voice of social protest and outrage as well as an ongoing attempt to develop new forms that would speak to a new society.

It is interesting to consider that Joseph Chaikin is traditionally associated with the trend toward collective creation and a theatre made of images brought forth from the "present" actor, whereas Shepard is associated with the writer's experiments with surrealistic streams of consciousness, language, and an attempt to forge myths from the texture of American pop culture. These are extreme positions, but in fact, in the 1960s, the work of both men shared similar concerns and techniques.

When Chaikin and Shepard met in 1964, both were at turning points in their lives. Chaikin had been in New York since 1955. He had joined the Living Theatre in 1959, where he performed a variety of roles in the repertory. His first Obie award was for his role as Galy Gay in Brecht's *Man Is Man* (1962). In February 1963, Chaikin and a group of actors and playwrights met at the Living Theatre to discuss starting a workshop to address acting issues not being considered by the directors of the Living Theatre, Judith Malina and Julian Beck. This group met sporadically through the spring of 1963 and reformed in the fall as the Open Theatre. When the IRS closed the Living Theatre during performances of *The Brig* in October 1963, Chaikin chose not to remain with the company when it went into exile.

Although Chaikin continued to act off-Broadway for the next few years (winning his second Obie in 1965), the Open Theatre workshop became his primary focus. Public performances by the workshop began in December 1963. During the 1964–65 season, the schedule of public performances increased. The company gave biweekly Monday night performances at the Sheridan Square Playhouse from February to May. The workshop was made up of some fifteen actors; critics Richard Gilman and Gordon Rogoff; playwrights Michael Smith, Megan Terry, and Jean-Claude van Itallie; and directors Chaikin, Peter Feldman, and Sydney Schubert Walter. The goals of the Open Theatre at this point were:

1. To create a situation in which the actors can play together with a sensitivity to one another required of an ensemble.
2. To explore the specific powers that only live theatre possesses.
3. To concentrate on a theatre of abstraction and illusion (as opposed to a theatre of behavioral or psychological motivation).[3]

The early performances of the Open Theatre were generally made up of group exercises and one-act plays, including van Itallie's "I'm Really Here" (October 1964), "The Hunter and the Bird" (October 1964), and "Pavane" (April 1965), and Megan Terry's "Calm Down Mother" (October 1964) and "Keep Tightly Closed in a Cool Dry Place" (March 1965). The 1965–66 season at La Mama emphasized plays rather than improvisations and exercises, and culminated with the production of Megan Terry's *Viet Rock* in May 1966.

A decision to open commercial productions of *Viet Rock* and van Itallie's *America Hurrah* caused dissension in the workshop, but both productions opened in the fall of 1966. Although neither production was an Open Theatre production, both were performed and directed by workshop members. These productions took time and energy from the workshops; consequently there was little workshop activity during the 1966–67 season. *America Hurrah* was a great financial and critical success with the result that critical attention and esteem was also directed to the work of the Open Theatre. In retrospect this period was the culmination of the first phase of the Open Theatre: these commercial productions provoked an internal crisis in the workshop that resulted in a restructuring and a refocusing of the work in 1967.

Shepard arrived in New York in 1963, the year of the founding of the Open Theatre. While working as a waiter at the Village Gate, he met an aspiring theatre director, Ralph Cook, who created the Theatre Genesis at St. Marks in the Bowery in July 1964. It was here that Shepard's first plays, "Cowboys" and "Rock Garden," were produced in October 1964. From then until his departure for London in 1971, Shepard wrote prolifically, and his plays were produced regularly in the off-off-Broadway theatres. Notable productions included "Chicago" (Theatre Genesis, 1965), "Icarus' Mother" (Caffe Cino, 1965), "Red Cross" (Judson Poets' Theatre, 1966), *La Turista* (American Place Theatre, 1967), "Forensic and the Navigators" (Theatre Genesis, 1967), "The Unseen Hand" (La Mama, 1969), and "Cowboy Mouth" (American Place Theatre, 1971).

Shepard and Chaikin met for the first time in 1964, at a dinner party. Shepard attended Open Theatre workshops, but made no contribution as a writer during the first phase of the ensemble's development. Shepard did, however, work on the screenplay of Robert Frank's *Me and My Brother*, which was shot in the winter of 1967 and featured Chaikin. And, often, actors and directors from the Open Theatre workshop were involved in productions of Shepard's plays.

The major change in the work of the Open Theatre in the fall of 1967 was Chaikin's decision to intensify his workshop schedule and concentrate on developing a full-length theatre piece working on material from the Bible. This piece, *The Serpent: A Ceremony*, with a text by van Itallie, opened in Rome in May 1968. The European tour was a great success, assuring the company grant support and making possible an extended American tour of the play. After reworking *The Serpent* for the American tour, the company began work on *Terminal*, which had its premiere on the company's second European tour in November 1969. Although the Open Theatre continued to produce productions from workshops not led by Chaikin, notably Peter Feldman's *Ubu Cocu* and a production of *Endgame* directed by Roberta Sklar, it was clearly the two full-company collaborative pieces directed by Chaikin that attracted the most attention and acclaim. Both *The Serpent* and

Terminal had nonlinear structures that allowed for a collage-like inclusion of disparate material. *The Serpent* included material from the Old Testament, biographical material provided by the actors, and contemporary events. *Terminal*'s theme was death and dying. In both productions the virtuosity of the actors was displayed. Each production was notable for striking visual images and a complex rhythmic and musical structure.

Shepard attended the workshops during the period of the development of both plays. He had, in fact, contributed some monologues for *Terminal* (published in *Hawk Moon*) that were not included in the final production. During this period he also joined a rock band, the Holy Modal Rounders. By 1970, Shepard had achieved fame and notoriety within the New York community. His plays were being published; Michaelangelo Antonioni had asked him to work on the screenplay of *Zabriskie Point*; and *Operation Sidewinder* had been produced by the Lincoln Center Repertory Company. He married O-Lan Johnson in 1969, and their son Jesse was born in May 1970. But his personal life was unsettled, and his affair with Patti Smith in 1971 was much publicized.

In 1971, Shepard decided to move to London with his wife and son, rejecting the whole New York scene. He remained in England, spending summers in Nova Scotia, until 1974. In London, he wrote *The Tooth of Crime*, arguably the finest writing he had done to date. It was staged by Charles Marowitz at the Open Space Theatre in 1972. Shepard directed the Royal Court production of his next play, *Geography of a Horse Dreamer*. It was during this period of exile that Shepard and Chaikin began corresponding.

The year before Shepard left New York, Chaikin had radically restructured the Open Theatre, reducing it to a company of six actors. This group reworked *Terminal* in 1970 and created two new pieces, *The Mutation Show* (1971–72) and *Nightwalk* (1973), which they toured throughout the United States and Europe.[4] Chaikin, however, wary of fame and fearful of the group's becoming institutionalized, decided to end the Open Theatre in 1973. He proceeded to develop individual projects for the next few years, notably Robert Montgomery's *Electra* (1974); van Itallie's translation of *The Seagull* (1975); *A Fable* (1975), a collaborative piece scripted by van Itallie; and Adrienne Kennedy's *A Movie Star Has to Star in Black and White* (1976).

During the winter of 1976, Chaikin formed a workshop, the Winter Project, which was designed to meet for an intense, but relatively limited, period to explore questions on acting and material of interest to Chaikin and the group. Underlying the Winter Project workshop were what Blumenthal called Chaikin's "deepest concerns": "the search for ways to express things on stage that people cannot generally express in their lives; the use of the body as well as the psyche to locate unfamiliar conditions; a recognition of the actor's presence along with the character's."[5] Chaikin's description of this workshop (Letter 17) emphasizes that "the idea was to investigate questions of telling and kinds of listening and maybe to find other ways to speak or sing thoughts and feelings." Shepard was one of the writers solicited for material and sent a song and speech. The planning of the second Winter Project was begun in the spring of 1977. Shepard was again asked to contribute. Although he had concerns about the position of the writer in the workshop—especially his geographical separation— he was intrigued by the proposed exploration of voice in relation to character and Chaikin's note that "the whole investigation has to do with meaning and *sound*." (Letter 17)

Shepard had, in fact, recently completed an "improvisational jazz piece," *Inacoma* (March 1977) at the Magic Theatre, which addressed questions similar to those raised by the Winter Project. After his return from London in the fall of 1974, Shepard settled in the San Francisco area. He developed an ongoing relationship with John Lion's Magic Theatre, where he directed "Action" and "Killer's Head" (1975) and *Angel City* (1976). The first of his family plays, *Curse of the Starving Class*, was written in 1976. And in the fall of this year, Shepard started work as an actor in a principal role in Terrence Malick's film *Days of Heaven*.

The first group of letters between Chaikin and Shepard covers a period during which both artists went through a series of important transitions in their work. It concludes at a point when Chaikin had begun a new series of workshop explorations and Shepard had started the first of a series of family plays that were to establish him as one of the foremost American playwrights. The letters reveal Chaikin's and Shepard's mutual respect and deep friendship as well as common concerns about theatre. Both men remained resolutely outside the mainstream in their work and were true to their own artistic voices. What surprises is the complimentary nature of these two minds: Chaikin's work with the actor to create emblems and rhythms for character parallels the poetic and musical structures of Shepard's writing.

Letters

1. London, n.d. [1972]

Dear Joe,

I was thinking about you so I thought I'd write and hope you'll write me back. Of all the people in New York you and Fred [Katz] keep coming into my head. I feel so stupid now that I wasted all the times I was with you, just talking or running into each other and me never feeling really there. I learned so much from you just by the way you live that I feel bad that I never gave anything in return. All your ideas and impressions seemed so powerful to me at the time even though I was never able to put them to any use, either in my writing or my life. I've come down to the understanding that everything I've done up 'til now has been in sleep. All my writing seems to have the same value as any product from any sleeping person. Of all the people working in the theatre you seem to be the most awake and, for that, the Open Theatre is to me like a religious group, at least it was when I knew it. Even though you were unhappy with some of the people, it seemed like the workshops always took on an air of worship. I hope everything's going good with you now and getting closer to what you want. I can't fucking believe this life! Remembering you, me, Jean-Claude [van Itallie], and Joyce [Aaron] on a beach in the fog is like a faraway dream. The way we came together and the way we grow apart. The times in Charlemont. You telling me that the moon really affects us "not in a mystical way either"—showing me the difference between the outdoors and the indoors. I don't feel sentimental about it, just amazed and a little sad that I was never present. Thanks for being around when I was, Joe. Say howdy to Fritz [Fred Katz].

Love,
Sam

2. *London, December 19, 1972*

Dear Joe,

Have you read any of Carlos Castaneda's books? It seems to me that much of the material in his books could be useful to your piece. He's written three: *The Teachings of Don Juan, A Separate Reality*, and his latest one, *Journey to Ixtlan*, which I find the most inspiring of all. His writings are a record of some ten years that he spent with a Yaqui Indian sorcerer in Mexico and Arizona. The sorcerer's name is Don Juan, and the books are journeys through his teachings. It's a really enlightening thing to read some of his words. Plus it shows very clearly the relationship between a person in search of knowledge and one who knows. One thing that Don Juan said that really struck me was: "Death is the only wise adviser that we have. Whenever you feel, as you always do, that everything is going wrong and you're about to be annihilated, turn to your death and ask if that is so. Your death will tell you: 'I haven't touched you yet.' "

I'm glad you're thinking of using some of the things I've written. There's another speech here that came to me. It's really great to be able to write passages and not have to worry about a form. . . .

I want to write a song for the piece [*Nightwalk*], but it'll take awhile yet. If you have more ideas, please let me know.

Love,
Sam

3. *London, December 24, 1972*

Dear Joe,

I'm a bit confused about the new direction of the piece. It sounds to me like the actors may be wanting to use their own language and ideas more. That's all right with me, but I need to know more about where I stand. I'm very eager to work on the piece as it develops, in whatever direction, but I don't want to be in the way of another kind of development. In other words, if what I've already written for you is enough for one particular area of the piece, and you want to develop something else with just the actors, then just let me know. If you need more written material in a different area, I'd really like to try whatever is possible. Right now I'm not clear on what you mean by a "creature." I realize you probably aren't either at this point, but maybe by the time this reaches you you'll have some more ideas. It would be very hard to write something from a creature without senses since that's the area of human experience where I find words come from. It would be something to try, though. I don't understand why the guide gets lost and the creature goes on without him. That seems to put them both on the same level, which seems less interesting to me. Anyway, let me know how things are going and whether or not you need any more writing.

Love,
Sam

4. London, January 18, 1973

Dear Joe,

Thanks for writing about the new developments. I think my main stumbling block is in how to find a space in myself for adjusting to a way of collaboration. I would much prefer it if you could tell me details of a style to write in when the opportunity comes for more words. For instance, it's very helpful to know that you need a sparse language more like poetry than a kind of prose— which is what I was using before. It seems obvious now that a more compact form of language comes closer to what the actors need. I'm still vague about the real direction of the piece, and I think the best thing for me to do now is to lay low until you need something specific. Once you have a better overall picture, then maybe new places for words will present themselves and I could add something then. Please keep me posted as it moves along. I still want to write something, but I think it's better to wait right now.

Love,
Sam

5. *London, February 22* [*1973*]

Dear Joe,

I finally got your book [*The Presence of the Actor*] from somebody over here and read it from cover to cover. I found myself feeling more and more fractured inside myself as I read it. I don't know if it was because of this time I'm in right now or what. Somehow the last few days I've been seeing in a different way. Like different layers seeing at different times. Your book helped me get inside a lot of the ideas I've been working on. . . . Most of me doesn't want to know the real experience of these ideas. Or what the ideas bring me to. But something new came from your book. Some kind of acceptance that I've got to let go into these worlds that I've resisted always. I know, right now, that all I can do is try to throw light on all my mysteries. I can't change anything now because I don't understand how I work really. It's a long struggle. I'd still like to keep some kind of dialogue going between us even though there's not much "theatre" writing left for me to do on the new piece. I know you're real busy, but if you have some time, I'd like to hear from you. Sometimes I feel I'm a long way from understanding the smallest thing. Other times I feel I understand everything. Most of the time I forget it's even a question. Your book helped remind me.

Love,
Sam

6. *Nova Scotia, August 21* [*1973*]

Dear Joe,

It was good to hear from you again. Another airplane letter. Every time I read one of those I have this picture of you writing the letter as you sit thousands of feet above the earth. I remember that conversation at Laing's about "will," and what I remember most is the feeling of being in conflict in myself. As though we were using the same words to describe different ideas. I was struggling to remain clear about my own idea while trying to make room for yours but somehow having this feeling of "wrong-ness. . . ."

Hope you can make it to Nova Scotia. We'll be here until about the 19th of Sept. Let me know if you can. If not maybe we'll see you in N.Y. when we pass through.

Your friend,
Sam

7. [Nova Scotia], September 4 [1973]

Dear Joe,

I got your letter and I feel sort of lost with it. . . . Right now I'm sitting in this big house alone at a long table writing to you. There's flies buzzing around the typewriter and outside it's a bright sunny day with the ocean glaring through the windows. In the back of my head is this idea I should start painting the front of the house. I've got this picture of you in New York reading this letter in your apartment. I come back here to myself. This sensation of being here and being not here at the same time. We'll be in New York from the twenty-first to the twenty-sixth. I'm going to try to see you sometime during that time. Will you still be there? Do you know if Peter Brook is still there? I really look forward to getting your letters and seeing you in the flesh again.

Love from us,
Sam

8. [London], January 26 [1974]

Dear Joe,

How are you? Thanks for the book. I've been reading through the parts you underlined whenever I get a chance. I find it heavy going and every once in a while a flash of something comes through. Mainly this feeling of this guy struggling with his reason and his intellect and his negativity, trying to formulate hidden things. A lot of what he says strikes home, like the part of earth being Hell and living is like being sentenced to a penal colony. . . . Everything comes out in fractured enthusiasm. When I sat down to write I wasn't even feeling enthusiastic. Anyway, I'm sending you a play I just finished. It's the first thing I've been happy about for a long time. Please write and let me know how you're doing.

Love,
Sam

9. [London], February 11 [1974]

Dear Joe,

I'm sitting here in the kitchen, early in the morning, smoking a cigarette and reading your letter. I'm really glad you like the play ["Action"]. It's very special to me. So far you're the only one who's seen it beside O-Lan. It would be terrific if you were to work on it. The kind of situation you describe for it (i.e., no opening night pressures, off Broadway, on Broadway, etc.) is exactly what's called for. If you want to continue with it in whatever way you find right I would be really happy. I want to be very careful with it. In writing it I found a whole new area. In moments it seemed possible to enter into the play and be inside it more completely. To hold each moment without becoming anxious about moving it forward to dramatic climaxes or resolutions. To let it sit in itself without force and have something come to it instead of always pushing outside itself. I don't know if I'm making it clear. I felt I became more of a receiver for the play rather than "creating" it. You know what I mean? The kind of production I would wish for is one that could provide the same kind of environment as the one it was written in. You're really the only one I know of who works in that direction. It needs a lot of time and development—investigation. Since I have no real place in New York anymore, I'd prefer it if you would find the kind of environment that was right for you and the people you'd want to play it. I know if I tell Toby [Cole] about the play that she would do her best to find the right situation, but she wouldn't be able to come up with it because she's kind of out of touch too, being in Italy. That's why I'd like to leave it up to you—if you're willing. Please let me know if you want to carry it further.

I've been directing my own play, "Horse Dreamer," here at the Royal Court. It's opened up lots of new doors for me. Constant work with people is a real opportunity to see things that are closed when you work alone. I've started to come back to the possibility of being involved with productions after a long time of non-involvement. It's incredible to feel yourself struggling in the same direction with others. Even to find myself uncertain in the face of questions from the actors. Been reading Peter's book [Brook, *The Empty Space*] too, which is a great help.

It must be strange for you now without a group to work with. Are you working on anything by yourself? . . .

Love,
Sam

10. *[London], March 22 [1974]*

Joe,

It's really OK if you want to change your mind about doing the play. Of course I'm disappointed about it, but I can understand your feelings, especially since the Open Theatre has ended. Please don't feel like our friendship hinges on anything like these kinds of decisions. I was surprised you wanted to do it in the first place although I secretly hoped for it. As far as Larry Sacharow goes, I'd really prefer to hold off on the whole thing now. I've been working more on the play and extending it some so I'd like time just to think about it some more anyway. Maybe I'll do it myself in California or something. In any event, something will work out. I hope things are all right with you. Please keep in touch.

Love,
Sam

11. *[California], August 14, 1975*

Dear Joe,

Glad to hear from you again. Events are going like a whirlwind for me out here. . . .

I'm working on several things. Just finished a screenplay, writing poetry, plays, and trying to form some kind of small company to work out a piece on "possession." All this is happening and makes me feel alive, then it all seems useless, and I go down into some kind of self-pitying despair. I see people around me struggling in the same way, and then it begins to look like a general condition of all of us. It's difficult to remain in the middle between these two and not take sides.

I'd really look forward to seeing you come to California and the possibility of working with you in any capacity. I think of you a lot and Fred [Katz] too. Do you see him anymore? If so, give him my regards. Write again when you get a chance.

Love,
Sam

12. Mill Valley, California, April 20, 1976

Dear Joe,

Good to hear from you. It looks like we're staying here in California through the summer due to lack of $. It's great here though. We're on twenty acres of land looking out over the bay. You could come out here and stay with us anytime. Just let us know when you're free. Lots of beaches nearby.

I've been real busy writing and taking care of horses. Go into rehearsal May 15 on my new play [*Angel City*]. Really looking forward to direction again. Please let us know if you think you can make it out here. It'd be great to see you.

Love,
Sam

13. [New York], n.d. [end 1976-early 1977]

Dear Sam,

Even though you haven't been around to be part of the Winter Project, it would be good to work together.

Joe

14. New York, April 6, 1977

Dear Sammy and O-Lan,

Have tried calling you by phone—no answer. Sam, saw "Suicide in B Flat" the other night. Made me remember and love you and reconnect. I wish I could tell you about the Winter Project and a few unresolved, but deeply rich studies of speaking and listening that it was about. Much more I wish you were part of it. Next winter we will start again, but this time aiming for performing. I will write you again to describe the structure in the great hope you will be interested to contribute to it, even by mail. I feel that some part of it would interest you.

Even though geography separates us and all the different circumstances that come up, I think of both of you often and as loving friends. If any chance of your being around these parts, please let me know. I will do the same.

Joe

15. New York, May 20, 1977

Dear Sam,

I haven't heard from you, but only about you, in a long time. Still, I think of you often.

Years ago I asked you to be part of a small group of international theatre people who might be able to create a context somewhere in this country that would enable plays to be done and experiments to be tried. Finally I think it may be coming about and I have included your name since you agreed once. It will be called "Center of Theatre Practice." The other playwrights are Jean-Claude van Itallie and Adrienne Kennedy so far. If bureaucratic details don't smother it, it may happen.

Also next winter we will go on with the Winter Project. This time taking it toward a modest performance. I wish so much I could talk to you about it. I think it would interest you.

Imagine one head out of which speak different selves. Each self is a voice, and I want very much to use records of yours. If we don't get a chance to meet and if you don't send new stuff, I would like to be able to go through material of yours and pick out a voice.

Apart from that, I miss you and send you love.

Joe

16. [Mill Valley, California] May 1977

Dear Joe,

Just got another letter on your Winter Project called "Thought Music." I'm a little confused as to the outcome of these projects. Last time I wrote a few things and sent them off to you. I never heard anything further about it. I think that time it was in connection with storytelling. This new project sounds very provocative, but I don't want to get all wrapped up in writing things for it if they just disappear. Hope you can understand my point of view. I always look forward to working with you in whatever capacity—so let me know how, when, and what to proceed with. Hope to hear from you soon.

Love,
Sam

17. [New York, May 1977]

Dear Sammy,

I got your letter and I will try to explain.

During the winter a bunch of people got together to tell words or sing words and to listen to each other. To see what could be heard in words spoken or sung. We tried also to examine qualities of listening. There was a big emphasis on the music in speaking-rhythm, melody and a lot of discussion about the degradation of language—that it's empty to use words like "love," "truth," etc., and yet one can't live without them, so, are there other words, code words, or ironies in language, or is it better to use them anyway accepting the pollution of language, etc. The idea was to investigate questions of telling and kinds of listening and maybe to find other ways to speak or sing thoughts and feelings.

This exploration was never performed outside the group of actors and composers and musicians and writers who came around and were part of it. No one told anyone what to do. We used each other as audience and said what we got. The performing became inseparable from the words, so there was really no way of describing to you how the song and speech you sent came across. They were beautiful to hear and we tried them a few different ways. No conclusions or formulas about approach, but a few very elementary things were revealed about the relationship between listener and teller. It's hard to go into by letter and the significant things you can probably guess.

Because I appreciate your writing a lot as do the rest of the people, we all wanted to do stuff of yours. The problem is geography. As we listen to each other and test material for what we hear, there is no way of sharing with you the immediate dynamic responses of the ORAL-AURAL experience. Most of the material we got into was inherited, as opposed to from living writers.

The reason you got the letter describing the next effort of the Winter Project is because everyone feels strongly about your words. How to collaborate in a fruitful way is really hard to figure out. These are the possibilities:

1. If you agree, we go through various things you've already written and create a "voice" taking a description here and an image there, a speech in another place. Although that sounds random, it would be done with care.
2. You send us anything you want and we try it and feel out its aliveness as a "voice." This has the one problem, that we would or might want to take the liberty of editing stuff, which is a delicate thing to do without you around. But again, if you felt OK about it, it would be done with care after listening together to see what was impelling to repeat again and again.
3. To conclude that the geography problem is too limiting and we can't satisfactorily do this kind of work together, which I would fully understand.

As far as Murray Mednick, I would be very glad if he sent anything he wanted to do, but it's very hard to describe all of the features to someone by letter when the whole investigation has to do with meaning and *sound*. I'd be glad if he felt like finding a "voice." It's a little like finding or locating an identifiable, recognizable, inner track that comes to consciousness in some repeated way.

Apart from this stuff—any way you want to relate to it is OK, I'm sorry for poor communication about it—life goes on for a while more. I miss you in my life. I would so much like to sit together on some grass or some beach and just be together.

Love,
Joe

18. *Mill Valley, California, May 23, 1977*

Dear Joe,

Thanks for the letter. I understand all the difficulties with space and communication along with the personal way of working that you have with the actors. All I was really curious about was what happened. We just finished an improvisational-jazz piece here called *Inacoma*, based on the Karen Ann Quinlan case, in which we explored some of the territory of voices which you describe. I'm very interested in writing some material around this impulse of an inner voice. It makes no difference to me if you want to edit anything I might send you. It's just words anyway. Right now I'm sort of in between things and I feel that this kind of writing would be very liberating for me to try. I'm still obsessed with this idea that words are pictures and that even momentarily they can wrap the listener up in a visual world without having to commit themselves to revealing any other meaning. The sounds and rhythms seem to support these images and bring feeling into it.

I'll try to work on some things around the ideas which you were talking about. I'll just keep sending you stuff as it turns up. Hope you can make it out here to the West Coast some time. It would be great to talk and hear more from you on this idea of an "International Theatre" group. Hope all is well with you. We all think of you a lot.

Love,
Sam

Sam Shepard:
Texts Written for
Nightwalk, 1972

Bones. Collapsed. Bones. Upright. At the top of the skeleton. I view the world. I view the world.

Collapsed. Bone. Not a man. Stand. A man. Upright. Grow. From the earth. Grow. From the earth. I grow. Up.

Was the world. In your head. In your box. Was the world. In your box. In your world. Was this world. Was this the world. In your head. What world. Was the world. Was the world. Like this. Like this world. Like this. Like this. In your box.

First thing in the morning, soon as I wake I have a dream of my death. In the moment of dying I leave my body, like a yellow exploding light. The light sees the life it had inside my body as less than a second in its own life.

Now I'm washing the dishes. Now I'm making the bed. Now I'm brushing my teeth. Now I'm thinking big thoughts. Now I'm lying. Now I'm driving the car. Now I'm walking the street. Now I'm falling asleep. Now I'm dead. Now I'm awake. Now I'm dead.

At the edge of the world. At the edge of the world it looks calm. At the edge of the world. At the edge of the world it breathes like a monster. It breathes like a deep fire. At the edge of the world I wait for a small thing. I wait in my nightmare. At the edge I'm waiting to fall. At the edge it's like any other place. At the edge of the world it's like a street corner. At the edge I'm engulfed in the street. In the rumbling earth. At the edge of the world it's like a calm still morning.

It's closing. At the edge it's closing. It keeps me from falling. Like a grandad. Like a father. It holds me. It keeps me protected. It lets me tremble. It lets me tremble. It holds me trembling.

[First version]

At the edge of the world. At the edge of the world. At the edge of the world. At the edge of the world. At the edge of the world. It looks calm. At the edge of the world, it breathes like a monster. At the edge of the world, it breathes like a monster. At the edge of the world, it breathes like a deep fire. At the edge of the world, I am waiting for a small thing. At the edge of the world, it's like a calm still morning. At the edge of the world, I'm waiting to fall. At the edge of the world, it holds me. At the edge of the world, it lets me tremble. At the edge of the world, it holds me trembling.

[Second version. Four lines from this text were incorporated into *Nightwalk* XVIII, "The Traveler's Speech."]

In my house the night moves in. The air's changed. Electric light. The water moves in the pipes. Somebody's taking a bath. I see myself on a ship at night staring out to the lights on the shore. One of the lights is me. Me in my house. Me on the ship at night staring out to myself in the house.

Below the sea is a blind fish. A long snake fish with blank grey eyes. Me in the ship is imagining him down there. He goes on sucking the bottom. I'm inside that fish. I sink, I sink. I don't want to die in my sleep.

The ship cuts me off from the house. The house from the fish. I'm inside that fish.

[*Nightwalk* VII, "The House and the Fish"]

JOURNEYMAN: I'm on a field as the sun rises. The long sweet grass licks my legs like snake tongues. A meadowlark keeps her distance, hiding her nest. I'm reminded of a dirty joke. There in the middle of the field with the sun rising a dirty joke plays on my mind. I shake it off. I got nothing against sex but I'm after something else. It keeps forcing its way in so I let it in. Tits and ass flash across my mind. The sky is golden pink. Like skin. A young deer bounds off toward the edge of the forest. The joke passes. It's replaced by a song. Piano ringing through my ears. I'm no match for my imagination. The damp morning oozes into my boots and soaks my socks. It's much different now from when I started out. It changes from moment to moment. Still I keep walking toward a clump of saplings. The idea of hot coffee and toast puts me in conflict. A wish to go back to the warm kitchen. Strange birds set up a song, warning each other of my coming. I'm a stranger here. Then everything leaves me at once. I'm left in an empty body. The sun splashes into my face. What was my reason for coming? I must've just wandered out here from my bed without a plan. Now I'm in the future of my day. I see myself having a good time later. I have to get this walk over with so I can have a good time. I turn to go back but it looks the same as when I started. The sun's just rising. The grass licking my legs. The dirty joke. I try to remember where I started. I go back too far. Before I was born. A star. An angel. A demon. Something glittering through time. This is a whole new day and already I'm lost.

JOURNEYMAN: This is a place I've never been but I can't take it as that. I have a word for everything. Without a word, a car is a strange thing. No stranger than a tree. A curtain opens on another world. A word comes and the curtain shuts. I try talking to the curtain. Making deals with it to open and show me more. It's only when I exhaust myself that it gives me a look. Even then it comes when I least expect it. Always suddenly, without warning. Then I'm off my guard. I have no way of knowing what I'm letting myself in for. The curtain's smarter than me. Sometimes it lets me into a false room where I'm proud for getting myself in. Here I roam around pretending to be a monk on my day off. I nod to my disciples. They cringe in all the corners but when I turn my back, they laugh. Even when I discover that the room's a fake I still pretend I'm new. I'm born again. At the end of a day of lying there's no telling how many chances I missed. Every one waiting to bring me home. Every one indifferent to my search. What's the search for, I'm perfect as I am. Everything's all right with me. There goes another chance out the window.

Sam Shepard:
"Ocean Song,"
The Winter Project, 1976–77

Down through the river time
All along the shore
I thought I knew the signs
Of all the days I wore
I wore it like a silver
I wore it like a gun
But now I see my time
Screaming on me like the sun

Great green is the ocean
Great dream in my eye
Cut loose this old ocean
It's got me til the day I die

Backwater don't lose me
Old moon's got me cold
Riptide's gone and choosed me
And left me my gold
I got no relations
In floods by the sea
Backwater don't lose me
It's only old me

Great green is the ocean
Great dream in my eye
Cut loose this old ocean
It's got me til the day I die

Notes

1. Kenneth Chubb and the editors of *Theatre Quarterly*, "Metaphors, Mad Dogs and Old Time Cowboys: Interview with Sam Shepard," *American Dreams: The Imagination of Sam Shepard*, Bonnie Marranca, ed. (New York: PAJ, 1981), 193.

2. Albert Poland and Bruce Mailman, *The Off-Off Broadway Book* (New York: Bobbs-Merrill, 1972), xi.

3. Program, *Aspects*, Sheridan Square Playhouse, December 16, 1963.

4. Shepard was a contributing writer to *Nightwalk*.

5. Eileen Blumenthal, *Joseph Chaikin: Exploring at the Boundaries of Theatre* (New York: Cambridge Univ. Press, 1984), 67.

-- 2 --

"Tongues" and
"Savage/Love"

The next series of letters deals with the development and performances of "Tongues" and "Savage/Love." The two pieces, collaborations between Chaikin and Shepard, were performed in San Francisco, acted by Chaikin and directed by Shepard. Under the combined title, *Tongues*, they opened at the New York Public Theatre in November 1979. Chaikin continued to perform the pieces throughout 1980 in Europe and the United States. They were videotaped by Shirley Clarke in December 1980.

Chaikin addressed the idea of collaboration in a letter he wrote to Shepard at the end of the summer in 1977, after returning from giving a seminar in Israel. Shepard replied that he felt "like writing in a new way now and have been thinking a lot about words emanating from many different sources in a character. Each one like a different voice without having to explain or justify their connection necessarily." [Letter 20] They were able to schedule a period of three weeks of work together starting in May 1978. Chaikin had performed the title part in Buchner's *Woyzeck* in 1976, and was interested in performing again. Working with Shepard would be like his own collaborative work with actors, but allow him to be the actor rather than the director.

During the eight months prior to his residency in San Francisco, Chaikin staged *The Dybbuk* at the Public Theatre (December 1977) and held a second Winter Project workshop. During the last week of rehearsals for *The Dybbuk*, Chaikin was hospitalized for a month. He suffered from endocarditis, an inflammation of the heart. Chaikin had a history of heart disease that dated from his childhood and had undergone open-heart surgery in 1974. Although at first he seemed improved after hospitalization, his condition gradually deteriorated. By the time he began work with Shepard in San Francisco, he had trouble breathing, and movement was painful.

This is the reason that the actor in "Tongues" remains seated in a chair throughout the performance.

Once Chaikin arrived in San Francisco, he and Shepard met regularly "over a period of about three weeks, each time changing location—a restaurant, a beach, a park, hotel rooms, a truck—then toward the very end, a theater."[1] Chaikin has described the work as such: "Every day we'd talk, and we'd work out one segment. We did it through both of us talking and his writing."[2]

Shepard's notebook for "Tongues" gives an idea of the process and the sequence of the work. They started on May 15, 1978, with a piece entitled "Song of Bone." It is an exercise in which Shepard wrote a phrase or word and recorded Chaikin's immediate response to it. This is followed by two poems not used in the final piece, "From the hotel" and "If I could be saved." The first day ends with the note "Story of rebirth." The notes from the next day are a draft of the first unit in the final text, "Story," and of the worker's and new mother's voices. On May 17 a "Chant-Song" was sketched in, but was not finally used. This is followed by several pages of fragmentary notes for possible voices and stories, some of which are developed later. On May 19 the "Hunger Dialogue" was drafted in an unelaborated form. The "Song of Skin" was also sketched in on this day. (The notebook is not dated after May 19.) The pieces continue as follows: "Invocation to Dead Voice," "Voice from the Dead," "Inquisition of Dead One," "Talking Letter," "Voice to One About to Die," "Talk Song," "Pompous Voice," "Leader's Voice," "Story of Myself," "Tongues," "Second Voice to Blind One," "The Thoughts About One's Death." The last page relating to "Tongues" is a production sequence with some music notes that Shepard used as a rehearsal/performance cue sheet.

The notebook contains preliminary texts for all the poems except the "Voice Calling for the Recognized Voice," which was mostly improvised by Chaikin. The typed rehearsal script follows the order of the notebook, starting with "Story." It does not include the "Chant-Song" or "The Song of the Skin" which were apparently not developed beyond their initial phase. It includes an "Imagined Interview with a Secret Voice" which was later cut and two poems that were originally the end of the piece, "Story of Myself" and "[Second] Voice to the Blind One." When these two poems were cut, the "Talk Song" was moved to the end from its original position after the "Talking Letter." The structure of the final piece follows the sequence of the development of the poems except for the shift of "Talk Song" to the end. Chaikin described the final few days before the first performances as follows:

> About three days before we performed "Tongues" . . . I got sort of cold feet about doing the piece. . . . I felt overly visible on stage. I hadn't performed for a while . . . so I said, "Why don't I put on a mask for the piece?" I tried to persuade Sam, and we tried it for about an hour, but it was no good.
>
> Then I said, "I think it should have music." He said, "It doesn't need music." It was actually very interesting without music. There were carved silences that were quite interesting. But I persisted. I said I knew a guy in New York who could do percussion very well, and who had all these homemade instruments. . . . Sam called him in New York, and the line was busy, so Sam said, "I'd like to do the music." So Sam did the music. . . . He literally composed the music with me as the voice.[3]

For the production at the Magic Theatre (June 7–11, 1978), Chaikin was seated in a chair draped with a black cloth. He wore a faded blue, collarless shirt, and an Indian blanket was draped across his lap, covering his legs. Shepard was seated with his back to Chaikin on a platform which elevated him so that his shoulders were at a level with Chaikin's. His percussion instruments and objects were arranged around him on the platform. Chaikin did not move from the chair. Shepard's arms could be seen. As Blumenthal noted, "Shepard invented and scored the various gestures (which, of course, neither he nor Chaikin could see) trying to give the sense that his arms, playing the instruments, were extensions of Joe's static body. The effect often was split-second images of a multilimbed Hindu god."[4]

The slightly less than half hour performance cannot easily be labeled. A sequence of poems and mini-dramas were enacted by Chaikin, who created a variety of different characters using the inner resources of the actor brought forth through the expressive voice. This concept has been constant in Chaikin's explorations from the Open Theatre workshop through the Winter Project. It is best expressed in the following passage from "Notes on Character . . . And the Setup":

> Ultimately acting is to be able to speak in the tongues of the tortured, assassinated, betrayed, starving parts of ourselves imprisoned in the disguise of the "setup." And to locate and liberate those voices which sing from the precious buried parts of ourselves where we are

bewildered and alone beyond business matters, in irreducible radiance.[5]

Shepard's description of "Tongues" is remarkably similar to this idea. He states that

> Joe and I approached the thing without any definite structure; all we knew was that we wanted to construct a piece that had voices coming up, sort of visiting a person. The age-old idea is that a character evolves along a line, and any deviation from that has to be explained somehow. But I feel there are many voices in a person, many different people in one person, so why shouldn't they have a chance to come out.[6]

The fact that the actor in "Tongues" uses no props or costumes or gesture (except facial gesture) emphasizes the concept of the character and his/her words embodied in the performer's voice. The two sequences of the "Voice Calling for the Recognized Voice" act as concrete examples for the creative process itself. And there are a variety of approaches to this central idea in the finished work. At the simplest level, a group of clearly distinct characters or voices are created: a worker hoping to get a better job; a woman who has just given birth; the voice of a distant relative in a letter; a pompous voice; and a public voice. A second group of voices are more abstract, less individualized. In the "Voice to Blind One," the focus is on the description of the room. The two voices in the "Hunger Dialogue" are ultimately absorbed into the idea of the all-consuming hunger developed in the final speech of the dialogue. And in the "Voice to One About to Die" the interest lies in the question "What does one say to someone who is dying?" The final poem, "Talk Song," is also a part of this second group of "voices."

The third type of "voices" in "Tongues" relates to what Chaikin described as being "the first idea, which was thrown away but is in the piece anyway." It was "to make up this thing about a person who died and had many other lives. And make a fantasy of lives."[7] The first piece, "Story," develops this idea, giving a collage of the "character's" life and confronting him with death through the "dream voice." This sequence and the sequence made up of the "Invocation," the "Voice from the Dead," and the "Inquiry to Dead One" at the center of "Tongues" seem to reflect some of Shepard's interests in trance states, moving out of the body, a kind of communication beyond death, and, finally, in "Talk Song" a communication between man and his natural environment. It is interesting to recall that the Open Theatre's *Terminal* dealt with the concept of communicating with the dead and with trancelike states of being.

The result, then, in "Tongues" is not a simple linear unity, although many critics have tried to find a central voice in the character of the first speaker, either as a dreamer or as a dying man reviewing his life. "Tongues" is, rather, a theatrical collage that incorporates aspects of Shepard's interest in the "super" or "supra" natural and Chaikin's theories about the way the actor works. Specific observations and ideas come from each. For example, the voice in the "Talking Letter" was based on a relative of Chaikin's; the idea of the "Voice to Blind One" came from an experience of Chaikin's, but the description of the room seems to come directly from a Shepard play; and the "Hunger Dialogue" was inspired by a real dialogue between Chaikin and Shepard that Shepard then expanded into a surreal reflection on hunger. The constant motif of confronting death relates to Chaikin's serious illness during the composition of the pieces.

"Tongues" in every way represents a collaboration of two very separate theatrical talents. Its performance clearly represents the distinction. Chaikin the actor faces the audience and brings through his body a dazzling variety of voice. Shepard the author is virtually invisible, his back to Chaikin. Yet his percussion accompaniment helps stress the rhythms of language and asserts his presence as the author who has created the rhythmic language of these poems.

"Tongues" was performed June 7–11, 1978, at the Magic Theatre in San Francisco. Chaikin then returned to New York, and Shepard prepared for the June 27 opening at the Magic Theatre of *Buried Child*, directed by Robert Woodruff. This play won Shepard the Pulitzer Prize in 1979.

Shortly after his return to New York, Chaikin underwent open-heart surgery. He spent most of the fall recuperating. Chaikin had reflected on the collaboration with Shepard and wanted to continue the work with him. They decided that the late summer of 1979 was the best time for both of them. Also, Joseph Papp had indicated interest in producing the new work and "Tongues" at the Public Theatre in New York in the fall.

Shepard was busy filming *Resurrection* on location in Texas during the first few months of 1979. And Chaikin's third Winter Project started in January 1979. Grants for this project required performances. The piece that was developed, "Rearrangements," was presented at La Mama in March. After this, Chaikin went to Israel to stage *The Dybbuk* for the Habimah Theatre.

In June, after Chaikin's return from Israel, the details for the next Shepard/Chaikin project began to fall into place. It was decided that the subject of the new collaboration would be "love and romance." They also decided that Chaikin would perform "Tongues" in case the new piece was not finished. Skip LaPlante (percussion and bass fiddle) and Harry Mann (winds) were engaged to create the music for the new piece, and LaPlante would learn Shepard's part in "Tongues." This would allow Chaikin to continue performing "Tongues" without Shepard and make possible the New York production.

Work began at the Eureka Theatre on August 16. The process was different from that of "Tongues." Shepard thought it would be better to work in the same place every day, sensing that a different work environment would affect the texture of the new piece and help make it distinct from "Tongues." Chaikin noted, "I improvised every day. I'd improvise in bed, sleeping; I'd improvise various kinds of things, and Sam sort of took it down, and edited it, and shaped it, and reshaped it, and then we'd both talk about the final shape."[8] In his introduction to the published text, Chaikin added:

> The first step was to choose the moments, and then to speak from within those moments. A "moment" could be the first instant of meeting the lover, or it could be the experience of lovers sleeping next to one another, with one a little bit awake watching the other one sleep. Unlike our approach to "Tongues," I would improvise around or inside a moment; Sam would write. We would later discuss and try things.[9]

By August 23, Shepard's notebook contained drafts of all the pieces as well as notes on a sequence for performing them. The first plan was structured in three movements. The second plan is the final order of the pieces. "Terms of Endearment" and "Babble (2)" have been inserted in this plan as they were added later. The title "Signs of Love" was crossed out and replaced with "Savage/Love."

The two weeks following August 23 were devoted to polishing the work, integrating the music and preparing the revival of "Tongues." Robert Woodruff, who had assisted on "Tongues," took over as director, although Chaikin has said that Shepard directed the pieces, and Shepard has claimed that Chaikin directed from "within." For "Savage/Love" Chaikin used a small platform with a pillow. Beverly Emmons created a variety of lighting effects in the small area used by Chaikin. Mary Brecht costumed Chaikin in a blue sweatshirt, loose-fitting gray pants, and a matching vest. The musicians were placed to the side, visible to the audience. The production played from September 5–9 as part of the Eureka Theatre Summer Festival.

In an interview a few days before the opening, Shepard and Chaikin described and discussed the new piece. "Savage/Love," said Chaikin, "concerns love and lovers, but it is hard to say exactly what it's about. It evokes certain things that have to do with love, but it doesn't try to define or explain it." Shepard added: "It's about the feelings that go with love, of one kind or another; the fact that love works on people and often winds up ravaging them. Some sections of the piece deal with love and some with the other side: terror, death, murder, separation, estrangement."[10] This unity of subject is the first element that makes "Savage/Love" distinct from the first collaboration. In "Savage/Love," Chaikin seems to play a single character in various "love moments." The fact that Shepard wrote on the basis of Chaikin's improvisations probably contributes to the feeling that we are hearing a single voice. Chaikin used a sleep motif in which the insomniac tosses and turns between the pieces. Harry Mann's wind playing add a bluesy tone that help unify the mood. In "Savage/Love" the music seems to grow out of the actor's work, but as an accompaniment, unlike "Tongues," in which it seems to be one with the words.

The dominant tone of the piece is discordant. Failure to communicate and disintegration of the relationship are the most prevalent motifs. There is a violence in Chaikin's speaking of many of the pieces that seems to grow out of the lover's frustration: this is, perhaps, the reason for Shepard's choice of the word "savage" for the title. The two sections called "Babble" most clearly objectify the failure to communicate. Communication between lovers breaks down in "Listening Faces," "Savage," "Acting," and "Hoax." A similar failure occurs in "Tangled Up," "How I Look to You," and "The Hunt," in which the lover tries to transform himself in the hope of making a connection with the other or imagined other. "Killing," which, like "Babble," has two variations in the production, is an extreme in which the disintegration of the relationship is seen as a kind of murder. "Absence" portrays this sense of loss in a sequence of surreal images. The pain involved in the failure of love that seems to be inevitable is why the lover watching the sleeping lover concludes, "I want to know I'll die before/We aren't lovers anymore."

Although the general tone of "Savage/Love" is harsh, it is not unrelenting. There is a sly humor in "Tangled Up," "Terms of Endearment," and "The Hunt." "First Moment" is a tender evocation of the awakening of love in a chance encounter. The final poem, "Opening," is an expression of communication achieved. And, like "Salvation," "Opening" presents an image of the sense of wholeness felt by the lovers.

After the San Francisco performances of "Savage/Love" and "Tongues," Chaikin returned to New York, and plans were finalized for his performance of the two works at the Public Theatre. The production, titled *Tongues*, was originally scheduled for a three-week run, November 7–26. Reviews were excellent, and the production was extended through January 21, 1980. Chaikin performed *Tongues* in Paris, Milan, and Rome in March and took the production on a West Coast and Canadian tour in the fall. His final performance of the two pieces was a series of taping sessions (December 18–22, 1980) in New York. Shirley Clarke directed the taping, using experimental video techniques.

What is, finally, most striking about "Savage/Love" and "Tongues" is the union of the two artists in the pieces. Their distinct voices and shared concerns are woven into a single piece of cloth. The result is a kind of chamber theatre that is often similar to what is now called performance art.

Shepard's program note for the 1979 production summarizes well the effect of the two pieces:

> In one way, both of these collaborations are an attempt to find an equal expression between music and the actor. They are like environments where the words and gestures are given temporary atmospheres to breath in, through sound and rhythm.
>
> Thematically, the two pieces offer small facets of bigger questions. Shifting impulses around ideas of voices, love, death, etc. we felt no urgency to tie these facets together or force them to tell a "story" but simply to present them as parts of a whole. Even so, connections somehow arise and a story seems to be told.[11]

Letters

19. New York, September 11, 1977

Dear Sammy,

I've been thinking of writing you, so now I am. Moving in a train that shakes.

I'm back from Jerusalem for a few days. I did a seminar there for directors and actors. I will do very few of those in the future, because: 1. I don't know what's useful for some. 2. It makes me talk too much in conclusions and my tone sounds too much like a professor. That tone stops thought for me when I hear it. After a lot of intense correspondence with the Israeli ITI [International Theatre Institute] about my not going because the government is selling arms to South Africa and my being persuaded to go— isolation as no real response—I went and stayed in Jerusalem. That's where the Moslems, Christians, and Jews all claim their center. Each religion starts there and has its historic memory there. It seemed like a source of imagination. Religion itself is such an amazing example of imagination. Of what's wished for and what's dreaded. Anyway, I can't describe it adequately, mainly because everything contradicts everything else and it's as commercial as it is awesome. Each group (and there are many, since each religion has such radically different parts within it) has its own existence, costumes, language, ideas of death, rules, and form. They are extraordinarily alike, even though the references are all original.

The people there are nervous, since they never know when there is a war. But they're surprisingly able to enjoy and have a free sensuality.

The political situation is a shifting of all kinds of historical, biblical, and economic changes that is determined to have an effect on the planet.

I worked with three different groups. Also I went to an Arab village and visited people there. And to a Palestine refugee camp. And stayed at a Trappist monastery, where they don't talk, and went to the extreme Jewish section for Sabbath service and ceremonies and went to an Arab mosque and met many people. It was really something.

Now I'm back. Besides *The Dybbuk* I'll be doing the Winter Project this year. I'm glad not to make plans beyond that, because it's so unclear what to do. What has vitality and which context is possible at all to work in. And I always need to find some kind of teaching job, which is the only way I can earn a living without selling my independence altogether. (At the moment I'm out of a job because the one I expected fell through, due to a city squeeze, but it doesn't take too much effort to find one.)

I want to bring up different ways I've thought about you lately and see if any of it seems realistic or appealing to you.

1. What if we work together on an as yet unwritten play of yours, for the theatre.
2. Or for radio.
3. Or what about writing a speech, or monologue or some kind of words that I would say as an actor in whatever disguise or disguises you would want to give.
4. Should I try to come out there for a few weeks at some point to try something together?
5. Do you want to come here?
6. Should we try something through the mail?
7. Should we put all of this off?
8. Is this a mistaken way to think of it?

It comes down to this for me: I'd sure like to work together, if we can find a context that would be creative for us both. In general I intend not to direct plays, unless I change my mind or unless it's something of yours that seems right. Performing material I care about is more appealing to me now. If we wanted to work together on something, Papp, for one, would want to help it happen.

Although it could work another way, these possibilities are apart from the Winter Project, which is a research project to explore verbal and musical language in order to see what experiences can be expressed in what ways—clearly.

My present schedule takes me to end of April.

Sammele, give my love to O-Lan and I would say Jess, but I don't think he'd remember me, even though I remember him very well when he was tiny and started to see everything.

This train bumping back to the city. I've been out by the sea on

Long Island and happily playing in the sun. Every possible day for the rest of September I'm going to go to the water.

Love,

J.

20. *Mill Valley, California, September 13, 1977*

Dear Joe,

Sounds like a penetrating time you had in the Middle East. It must be a strange sensation to be in the midst of all that convergence of cultures and religion.

Your idea of working together is very exciting, but the geographical gap between us really presents a problem. I don't feel I'd really like to attempt a collaboration by mail. There's something too stilted about it and it doesn't afford the opportunity to speak directly about our interests. I don't even have a specific subject in mind—only an impulse that we might find something if we could have a period of talk and exploration.

Is it possible for you to come out here when your schedule is finished in April? I've been working here at the Magic Theatre in San Francisco as the "playwright in residence" for about three years—directing my own plays with the same group of actors—most of whom I like a lot. Also some jazz musicians—saxophone, piano, drums, etc. I'm at a place right now where I don't want to just go on directing my own work, but I'm not sure what new direction to take. Would you be interested in coming out sometime in May and working together for a period of a few weeks—either incorporating other actors and musicians or not—you acting—some kind of loose collaboration? O-Lan would be real interested in working together with us too. We could get you some money through the Rockefeller grant that the theatre receives and you could stay here with us or we could find you your own place—whichever suits you best. We may have to consider performing something out of what's developed at the Magic Theatre in order to qualify for the Rockefeller money. In any case it would be on a very limited basis of three performances a week or something. The theatre is very small—fifty seats and right in downtown S.F.

I feel like it could be a very exciting time, where we could exchange lots of information and explore some new kind of territory. I've been discovering all kinds of things about my own writing but still feel it lacks some kind of direction. I'm also going to be working with a theatre for the blind in the city. I'm interested in the whole process of visualization. What happens when we visualize pictures to ourselves—inside?

Please let me know soon whether you think your coming out here is a real possibility. It would be great to see you again.

Love,
Sam

21. [*New York, mid-September 1977*]

Dear Sam,

Yes, I would like to come out there for a few weeks and work together on something or different things. It sounds like a good thing to do. How about approximately four or five weeks in May or June or even later if that's more convenient to you. For me it's OK any time starting May.

I feel fine about going in whichever direction—with the company of musicians and actors that you are presently working with or not or a different way—the only thing is to leave open some part of the structure so we can hope to make discoveries together. I understand that there has to be some kind of structure. I would like a chance to perform some of your words because I want to express out of my own voice and body and breathing, but I couldn't direct any part I performed in. I could, as a director, step out on any other part. Essentially it doesn't much matter to me what function I play in it as long as we get a chance to put some questions to the stage and play around with some material.

I would like to stay in town, because I can't drive and wouldn't have mobility if I stayed at the ranch, but I'd love to visit your place and be able to stay over sometime.

I would be glad if O-Lan were part of this project—study—experiment—whatever it's called. I feel fine about performing it publicly in whatever arrangements the theatre works out.

I also have a lot of questions which direction to go. So I'm just going ad hoc. But more important than ideas to work with seems to me the people to work with. So I would be glad for a collaboration with you.

Let me know and I'll let you know any change or further specifics to do with arrangements. Is there something I need to do about the Rockefeller thing—a letter? What is the best period for you?

Just as much as I would like to work together, I look forward to being together.

Love,

J.

22. *Mill Valley, California, September 29, 1977*

Dear Joe,

It's really great that you can come out here. The first week in May is what I was thinking in terms of. How's that for you? What I'd like to do when you arrive is just talk about some of the directions you are thinking in terms of and find where we might coincide. I really feel like writing in a new way now and have been thinking a lot about words emanating from many different sources in a character. Each one like a different voice without having to explain or justify their connection necessarily. Within that kind of framework there could be very recognizable "everyday" relationships to return to. Mainly I'm seeing this as a compact project with just you and O-Lan and maybe one musician. If you could tolerate me writing and directing, that's the way I'd like to go. I don't have any structure at all in mind other than the imagined vision of you and O-Lan in a space with sound. We could take that as a ground zero and work from there. I do like the idea of singing, too. Harmonies, spoken rhythms, etc. . . . I really hope this all comes about as we've never really had a chance to work directly with each other before.

I spoke to John Lion, who is the artistic director at the Magic, and he says the theatre could give you a two-thousand-dollar fee plus a plane ticket. Does that sound fair or would you need more? I really don't know what the going scale is for this kind of thing. He's also concerned about the length of time you'd be here. Is four or five weeks enough to explore the material we find and also perform it? I'm sure we could arrange some way to condense the performance time, but I'd hate to push ourselves into any kind of pressure during the discovery. What's your thoughts on this?

We're also going to be moving to a new house around Xmas time which is closer to town and not so remote as the ranch. You might like staying there better, and I don't mind at all driving you into the city when you want to go in. This can all be worked out later.

Please let me know if you have any new thoughts about all this.

Love,
Sam

[On back in Chaikin's hand]
    four to six weeks
    audience observing process

23. [New York, October 1977]

Sam,

How to structure the
$\begin{cases} \text{investigation} \\ \text{workshop} \\ \text{rehearsal period} \end{cases}$

What do we call it—I refer to it as working together—seems to me just to see what might bring more discovery and what will be limiting. So far, as you describe it, it sounds to me like there wouldn't be any impediment. I feel OK about your directing, O-Lan and a musician you choose, and just starting somewhere. If you want to add any other elements or change something or think about a particular region of thought, let me know so that I might be able to incubate with it. If I think of any particular images or ideas or feelings, I'll write you. Mostly, it seems good that it should be very minimal, so that things could come up and then we could try to guide what comes up, and argue and make some choices and finally perform something in a stage of work. Maybe we want it to be a perishable thing and end there. Maybe to change or develop it or not. Seems better not to make designs beforehand on what it would turn into. It would surely reduce the creative possibilities.

Practically—I can come as of mid-May. At the moment I am booked here until May 12. I could come immediately after that.

I know that four or five weeks is not long, but who can be so specific about how long any process should be or if we worked together for fifteen weeks that it would be better. There's that theory that things take as long as the time given. I know that theory falls apart sometimes, but a lot of occasions, it doesn't. In any case, my personal reservations about a longer time come out of an old problem of mine in staying away for a long time. Those are the directions of thoughts and feelings I have regarding the period of time. I'm open to rethinking.

Mostly the chance to try voices from different sources, the harmonies and rhythms that you refer to—for me to use my own voice and breathing rather than trying to evoke something from someone else—what I mean is, this really sounds like a good basis for our working together where we could both try ways. I look forward to it. I would like, for example, to try voices, tones, and intentions of speaking within the voice and hear what is understood by it. (This is an example of getting caught up with something which has to be tried and not clear when described.)

For the rest—money, place, etc.—it'll be arrangeable. Should I write to John Lion directly? I'll accept whatever he can offer, but because I'm poor I need to ask for the maximum. Most of what I do doesn't pay—or almost nothing. A thousand dollars sounds OK with a ticket. If he could also provide an apartment for the period, it would be simpler. If not, I will manage. But I can't ask you to drive me in and out of town. I wouldn't feel comfortable with that.

The Public Theatre is doing your play right after *The Dybbuk*, which I'm just about to go into rehearsals for. That sounds like a work I really want to see. I've never read it, but I've heard it described by different people. Are you coming in for that?

Also, if you want me to read anything particular or think along particular lines before May, let me know. Or do you think it's better to be more unprepared?

Love,

J.

24. *Mill Valley, California, October 17, 1977*

Joe,

I think we both have the same basic sense of the way we want to approach this thing. It seems like the best thing to do now is wait until we come together and start from that point rather than build up too many notions ahead of time. We can send each other ideas from time to time in the meanwhile if you want to—small flashes or inclinations—whatever you want to call them.

I'm going to be doing a two-week laboratory-workshop with Grotowski in November and looking forward to it a lot. I know you've had experience with him before, but this is a first for me.

We've just bought a small house here in town and we're in the process of making the move. I've been cutting down blackberry bushes and putting up a fence for the dogs. I like living out here a lot, although I'm always returning to a feeling of dissatisfaction no matter where I am.

Say hello to Fred if you see him.

Love,
Sam

25. *New York, January 8, 1978*

Dear Sammy,

I'm writing to you from a little hospital room, where I am leashed to an intravenous thing. I've been here for twenty-seven endless days and nights so far, but I'm supposed to get out in about two weeks. They've warned me that in the next three months, there is a chance of complications. So I have to wait it out. I don't foresee any conflict with our working together, which I continue to enjoy knowing. This sudden, terrible illness I am now finishing is called "endocarditis." John Portland had something just like it.

The nights and days move into each other like one continuous misery. It's easy to say it now, because it's less and it's ending. I keep saying to myself—what is there to learn from this kind of suffering? It's constant pain and maximum discomfort, but sometimes I feel I transcend all of it. To my disappointment it is never by will or wish or resolve. And sometimes I get a laugh.

I read a lot, watch TV even more, and listen to music practically all the time, since I am unable to move around at all in this period.

What funny, always unexpected, turns life takes. I have never found living so wonderful as in the last couple of years or so. And I have never understood so little.

Soon your play will be on in N.Y. in the same theatre where I worked on *The Dybbuk*.

Sammy, I send my love to you and O-Lan.

Joe

26. *Mill Valley, California, January 11, 1978*

Dear Joe,

What a drag that you're in the hospital again. I heard about it through my director, "Woody," who was at Papp's theatre and got the word from them. I had no way of getting in touch with you, but I'm glad to hear you're coming through it all right. I always feel helpless when someone's sick and slightly guilty for having the good luck of being healthy myself. It's terrible you have to keep going through these sessions with pain. I don't know how you take it. I'm very chicken when it comes to anything having to do with doctors and the smell of medicine.

If it becomes impossible for you to travel when a time comes for us working together—then maybe I could come out there. I don't know yet, but we could think in those terms if you need to be careful with your body.

I've been reading the new Castaneda book called *The Second Ring of Power*. Especially the chapter called "The Art of Dreaming." This has been an inspiration to me along the lines I've been working on, which has to do with a feeling of separation between my body and "me." This feeling is only periodic and comes in small flashes but seems to act on me like a sudden insight into another world. . . .

I've been living a very cloistered life lately. Planting trees, identifying birds (a new interest), taking long walks with my dogs on a marsh right near here. I don't know how it came about, but everything I ever wished for is coming true. Jesse is a tall seven-year-old kid now and starting to pick up teenage slang already. His biggest fixation is the movie *Star Wars*, and he crashes through the house all day in disguise as different characters. I've been reading all kinds of books now that I avoided in my "hipper-sixties period," when I was too cool to read. Authors like Joyce and Conrad and Faulkner. Incredible worlds. Writing, for me, has become more and more difficult, and I tear up four plays for every one that I turn out. I'm still as uncertain about my motives for writing as I was when I started. I guess it's mainly an obsession or, at worst, a habit I can't get rid of.

O-Lan's into music now more than ever and spends a lot of time working out pieces on piano, sax, and flute. Our new house is great for space—since there's five of us living together. I sure hope you can stay with us awhile if you come out here.

Please keep in touch and have a strong recovery.

All our love,
Sam

27. New York, January 13, 1978

Dear Sammy,

I can't use my right hand for the next couple of days so Rhea [Gaisner] is writing this letter which I am speaking. I'm feeling much better and much stronger and will soon be out of the hospital.

There is a possibility that I'll have to have some more medical attention in the next couple of months after which I should have no problems relating to illness. When I wrote you before I was feeling heavy—now it's different. That's why I'm writing you this letter to let you know that it's different.

I am glad for our chance to work together in May when you will be composing words which I will perform.

Love,
Joe

28. New York, February 3, 1978

Dear Sammy,

Writing to let you know that I'm home now for ten days and practically all of my strength is back. I've begun a modified schedule and expect it to be full in a week. I'm not quite out of the woods, though, because the doctors tell me that it takes about three months before they can say that there are no "complications." So I get checked up once a week now.

Medical bills are astronomical. I can't believe that recovery is so expensive. I will be trying to get little talk gigs to help. In Los Angeles I have had some invitations for a one- or two-day thing. So now I'll be setting that up on the way to San Francisco.

If you get a chance read Kierkegaard's *Either/Or*, volume one. It's full of surprises.

It was wonderful to hear from you in the hospital.

Love,
Joe

29. New York, March 17, 1978

Dear Sammy,

Talked to John Lion by phone. He has arranged for me to stay in someone's house near the theatre. I'll probably start there and then move once I find a very private apartment somewhere else, so it seems to be in control.

I guess the word is out that we're doing this because I've gotten mail from actors who want to be in it, directors who want to observe, and a journalist who wants to do a story. So far I've put everybody off about everything.

New York is just starting to thaw and I am inching back to health, which I've missed so much. I feel like a plant which is just about to revive as spring comes.

My love to you,
J.

30. *Mill Valley, California, March 20, 1978*

Dear Joe,

Thanks for the tapes you sent. I got very influenced by your reading of "How It Is" by Beckett and took off on a flurry of writing which I guess I'll show you when you come out. It may not be at all what you have in mind, but the sense I got from the reading of inner voices engaged in different attitudes toward the body which is on a journey is what really moved me. As though the body is a vehicle and the passengers aren't all that willing to be travelers—they have arguments, discussions about their destination—take side trips—rest—get bogged down—then continue—then get a glimmer of where they're going.

Anyway, I'm trying to keep it from becoming a play. Just voices in search. Hope you're getting much better now.

Love,
Sam

31. *New York, March 30, 1978*

Dear Sam,

The idea of two voices, or more, or however it turns out sounds like a good starting place. I would enjoy looking for the voices. I feel sure that whatever material has meaning to you will be something which I will be able to find an inroad into as an actor. I look forward to finding ways to find a common focus. I look forward to performing words of yours with my voice and mouth and face.

In your plays the only thing that made me feel separated, even when I intensely admired and felt close to them, was the Americanness. The reason is because I have *always* felt like a foreigner here. I don't know how to account for it altogether; it is the culture which is most familiar to me, and still I feel like a refugee. I have often felt that the American contexts of your plays are among the strongest features of them and are like no one else anywhere, but temperamentally that made me feel distant, as everything American almost does. On the other hand, I would enjoy playing it the way a period and foreign play is—like a masquerade.

My body is not yet secure in this healing period, but I'm working fully, and I'm told I have only a few more weeks of these off-the-wall symptoms. . . .

What matters is that spring is slowly arriving and, even in N.Y., crocuses and tulips have started to push up from the ground while down the street some snow has not melted. New York seems, in contrast, like a zoo with driven animals. It's often amazing but never restful. Continually frantic. I'll be glad to transfer out of it for a while.

I can't wait to see Jess. My memory of him is as a wonderful, loving child. He must be very different, but he had a tender character I hope has grown with him.

It's late at night. I'm almost asleep. Not sure about anything.

Love,
Joe

32. [*New York, April 1978*]

Dear Sam,

I've been working with a group of musicians and actors under second and last season of the Winter Project. It's just a study group. That is, a questioning group—no productions. Now it is over. I'm tying up loose ends and soon getting ready to go to San Francisco.

It occurs to me that my letters to you are written out of very contrasting moods. My medical situation has been so strange and fluctuating and, with it, my moods. One doctor says that there's nothing wrong with me and the other says there's plenty wrong. Suddenly I sever any future and next day I'm planning what I'll do when I'm fifty-eight. I start rehearsing my death, which is nothing new to me, except the elements are always different. The odd thing is that I feel happy or depressed, but it has nothing to do with the prognosis. I feel liberated sometimes and full and deeper when the prognosis is grave and other times vice versa. If my letters to you are peculiarly different in tone, it's partly due to this strange fluctuation, since my immediate next plan has to do with coming out there. The truth is that all of living is so vivid and ephemeral and inconclusive and vast that it's hard to take.

Because my medical bills are for the very rich and I have recently had the luxury of illness, I have to do a gig here or there, which means give a class or make an appearance or a talk publicly. I am coming to San Francisco on the evening of the 14th on a plane from Dallas, Texas, where I will be stopping from New York to do a class.

Once I am in San Francisco I will also do a class or workshop or something. I'm telling you in advance so that you won't be surprised if you hear about it.

Also, lately I've been finding a lot of people doing papers on me and other kinds of publicity things. I get rid of ninety-seven percent of it and I do a little. A few people want to do a story of our working together or interviews, etc. I've said no to anything that implicates you, because I don't know how you feel about that. Sometimes I feel I have to protect myself entirely from any publicity and sometimes I feel fine about it—most of the time I feel protective in New York.

I've been calling you on the phone with no answer, but will try more.

Love,
Joe

P.S. I thought more about your idea talking to the body and such. It's more and more compelling.

Remember when the theatre used to have a lot of ghosts as characters.

33. Mill Valley, California, April 21, 1978

Joe,

Please let me know your flight number, airline, and time of arrival on the 14th—I'll come out and pick you up at the airport.

I understand your fluctuations in moods very well, if only from the point of view of someone not faced with such drastic physical conditions.

I tried to write you before this about some writing I've been doing in connection with us working together. I stopped because it all felt after the fact. I have put a lot of words on paper which seem to have come out of rhythmic impulses more than anything. Sort of like music, I guess. I can't even explain what the words are about, but they have a feeling of incantation or something. Chant-like. I'll show it to you when you come.

If there's any chance of me taking part in some of your classes you'll be doing out here, I'd definitely like to.

Love,
Sam

[June 7–11, 1978. "Tongues" performed at the Magic Theatre, San Francisco.]

34. *Mill Valley, California, July 28, 1978*

Dear Joe,

I'm so glad you're alive and going on! You sounded so positive on the phone—although a little weak. Afterward I just broke down. I don't even know why. I don't cry easy, but I feel this strong emotional attachment to you. As though I know you in some way I can't express. I never felt it was easy to talk—that's one reason I write, I guess.

I saw the film *Kaspar Hauser* by a German guy [Werner Herzog]. It's very beautiful. He says things like: "Nothing lives in me but my life" and "When I came to this earth I suffered a great fall." I finished the Beckett book finally, which I'll send you if you still want to read it. The work we both did while you were here is still alive in me somewhere. It was a great influence you brought.

I may be in N.Y. before Xmas and I'll come to visit you. Please let me know how you're doing when you can. I hope you get strong quickly.

Love,
Sam

35. *New York, August 9, 1978*

Dear Sammy,

I'm home now and in the second stage of recovery. I haven't left my apartment yet. Looking out into the daylight, I keep wanting to go into it and I will be able to in a couple of days, I think.

There was one complication from the surgery, which is a certain kind of irregular heart rhythm. It would be dangerous except for a medication that effectively steadies the heartbeat. I will have to take this medication for three months. After that the danger is over.

I'm encouraged by feeling stronger each day and because I can breathe now without effort. But there's still pain.

If all continues smoothly I will be increasing activity more and more, and by November I will supposedly be able to do anything. They still say I can go into competitive sports. I have never had the faintest desire to go into competitive sports until now. Just to test it.

My heart size became so enlarged that every beat shudders my chest and vibrates in my ears. I feel like a time bomb. But that too is getting better as my heart will slowly shrink.

Again I've been plunged into an encounter with mortality. Mine and everybody else's, because this kind of illness shows how common a situation it is and how hidden. I want to live deeper. I don't know how.

Sammy, your letter went inside me and affirmed a closeness and brotherhood I feel with you. At such a time as this, it's strengthening and love-giving.

J

Tonight George Bartenieff is going to drop off a script. I hope I can be helpful to Woody [Robert Woodruff] on casting. I don't know too many actors anymore, but I know some very good ones, and I'll see if any is suitable to the play [*Buried Child*].

As for the Beckett book, send it if you like it very much.

36. *New York, September 30, 1978*

Dear Sam,

Sometime back you wrote that you might be coming to New York, but I don't remember when.

Finally I'm feeling stronger and most of the time I'm able to do anything I need to.

Would you like to do "Tongues" together for just a few times when you come over? I would like to do it for the pleasure of it. On the other hand, it's also fine to leave it as having been done and realized. I thought about it and so thought that I might as well write and see how you thought. If we were to do it again, I would want to find a way to see you. I found during the radio performance that certain musical values were possible that weren't before. Or maybe there's another way to find those points. You were finding them by ear, but I think they would be still more vivid shifts if we both could find them sometimes.

If this is not a good time to do it again, or if it's better to not do it again, I want to repeat, that's OK with me.

Wish we could meet and talk about this and that.

The season here is changing and it has a different beauty and a different life. Meanwhile New York seems more hysterical and feverish than ever. And I'm in it.

I'm glad to be alive. Another reprieve. It was so extreme. Only now am I finding any perspective.

Love,

J.

37. *New York, October 16, 1978*

Dear Sam,

When I got your letter describing the way you feel at home, it reminded me that even when I saw you in June, you seemed more at home than ever before. If you have a choice, I don't think you should come to N.Y. yet. It's feverish here. There are many compensations, but it takes adapting to. It's better that you come when you feel restless or have some other reason. You and I can find another way to work together at some other time. I would be glad to come out there again, when I have an open schedule. . . .

I'm still recovering in this slow, unsteady but certain, way. I've been teaching a few times a week. A part of me is waiting until my body is steady again. People tell me I look well. I look better than when I was in S.F., since I was sick then. But my hair is grayer and thinner.

Outside N.Y. the leaves are changing. It's amazing how they change into these vivid, extreme colors, before they fall.

Love,

J.

Before mailing this letter, Channel 13 called saying that they want to produce "Tongues." That it could be done within a two-day period and whether or not you were coming to N.Y. I told them that it was uncertain whether or not you were coming in. I'll ask them to contact you directly.

It's a small point, but I don't think of "Tongues" as a written collaboration at all. I feel that you are the writer altogether. That you wrote it for me in a way. That performing it has been collaborative, but the writing not. I enjoy knowing that with your writing talent and our common performing work is how it came to be.

38. New York, December 28, 1978

Dear Sam,

Good to talk to you. I was surprised to feel your absence so much when you were inaccessible. Please know that I trust your independence to choose the extent of your privacy and non-privacy. I will be glad to not call you or even to not write to you, if you preferred. I take the same liberty with people that I feel an affinity with. To whatever extent possible, one should compose one's lifetime. It isn't a lot. My closeness to you is continuous and I feel that from you. Different times bring out different needs to do with privacy, I find.

Anyway, if you are not in this privacy or wanting it with me, I want to check with you about the following:

I would like very much to work together again because it seems that it would be possible to develop things out of our last experience.

Also because one of the things I really don't like in the theatre are the numbers of people involved in any project. I would like to work in small, small groups where maybe it is possible to find ways to transmit. If you want to, we can do it in one of two ways. Either through the mail and telephone or I can come there again—either in the summer or next winter. It is ridiculous to plan so far ahead, when nothing can be known about the future. On the other hand, my schedule is closing in and I have to either go with plans on hand or make other ones. This is a very unspontaneous profession.

I'm now on a train that shakes a lot so if my writing gets funny, you'll understand. I'm on my way to New York from Charlemont, where I went for a couple of days to be in the country.

I read "Tongues" to a group of people in N.Y., completely informal, some friends, students. The reaction was so enthusiastic and I took a joy in doing it—more than I expected. It's good when something is repeatable. I explained that the dimension of music and some nonverbal voice with music would be missing and couldn't be described. And it was missing very much. For me it felt like half the piece. As I mentioned to you on the phone, I really appreciate the sound and music that you composed and performed. It was excellent. In some cases it opened up the words and images. In some cases it accompanied and other times it took on a size that put the words of the character in a perspective, making the character small scale in a vast perspective. At the same time, the text alone, without music, has a very great range and substance. It was eventful for me to speak it (I didn't really perform it) and to experience the shifting focus of the listeners.

Unless you tell me otherwise, I would like to do it again for a small, informal, nonpaying group, sometime at the end of January. For the most part my energy will now be going into the Winter Project, probably its last year. This time we have to do it publicly. I feel that we've barely begun to find the questions, but something will be performed in March. Immediately after I will be going to Israel to direct *The Dybbuk* in Hebrew. Let me know if, when, or how we should coordinate together. Otherwise I'll be scheduling other things. It's OK with me to put it off for a long time or to try to do it within the year.

I saw Grotowski. We had a long and full day and evening together. Now he is going to the woods and "softly disappearing" until 1980. He will then come out—"If I live," he says—and move around the world with a group of people from different civilizations. He invited me to come to the Polish woods and visit or even stay. I know I wouldn't stay, but maybe I'll visit if I can work it out with time. He got me a copy of a book called *The Informed Heart* by Bruno Bettelheim. He said it was very important to read it at this time and that he's giving it to the few people that he works with there in Poland. It's very painful to read. I'm halfway through, finding it hard but necessary to continue. I'm telling you this in case you want to get it. It's easily available in paperback.

Music is my great friend and consolation. Maybe I'll send you a record of something. . . .

Love,
J.

39. *New York, January 15, 1979*

Dear Sam,

Tried calling you. I think I miswrote your new number in '79 address book, so I will write these two questions.

1. J. Papp called me. He would like to do "Tongues" or a new piece or both. He asked me to call you about your interest. He suggested working in July. If you are up for New York around then, I can be free. Let me know or call him directly.

2. I'm rehearsing with the Winter Project. The obligation we have for this last year of it is to perform something in March. It's really a research thing and I wish I could go into some questions much more intensely and deeply. But since we have to go public (performing the month of March at LaMama), we're trying to figure out what to do. The group is made up of Ronnie Gilbert, Paul Zimet, Tina Shepard, Joyce Aaron, a couple of other actors who I don't think you know and a couple of musicians. I've told you some of the questions and ideas we are working with. I'm asking you, for the group, if we can take small parts of "Tongues." The actors are very drawn to it. There is no way of doing it intact in this situation, because I'm leaving for Israel mid-March. If that doesn't feel right to you, there's no problem. We'll find other material or it will be less verbal. It comes down to the fact that "Tongues" includes some of the best writing around and we've been looking.

These letters are out of sync because of time and airplanes. Call or write to me on the two above questions.

Wishing you well.

Love

J

40. New York, February 14, 1979

Dear Sammy,

Got your letter. Papp is pressing me for arrangements with you, as though I represented you. I told him to work it out directly with you. . . .

Providing things are fairly quiet in the Middle East, I will be leaving for Israel in about a month and I will return around June 1. I would love to work with you sometime this summer and I will contact you once I'm back, or I'll be hearing from you.

The idea of music and musicians is very appealing to me.

Hope it goes well for you, my friend.

Love,

Joe

41. New York, March 12, 1979

Dear Sammy,

I got your letter. It's hard to visualize you in the cinema world, but I particularly appreciate that kind of incongruity. . . .

When you and I get a chance to work again, the single main condition is that nobody else determines how it goes. Papp would be OK with me and I know he would not interfere. Still, he's not the only person who could provide a context.

I just finished a production here. It's a romantic piece called "Rearrangements." It seemed to go in its own direction. It's a comic piece—the lightest I've ever done. My feeling about it is that it's one third of a whole, but we stopped and closed it in order to perform it. Working on it was fun, but arduous in LaMama's cold loft without money enough to live on. For me it's not a problem because I can always do a teaching gig to supplement income. For others involved, it's very hard.

I'll be going to Israel about March 29 or 30.

It's clear to me that no single direction in the theatre is possible. Not only because there is no track to take in the theatre, but this era has forced many questions on everyone. Nothing is in the place it has been and it feels so much like the end of something, while it is also the beginning of something unimaginable. It's a very exciting, wonderful, dreadful time. The difficulties in the theatre are symptomatic of many things going on.

I have a couple of weeks before I go. I think what is relaxing, nourishing, restorative. It's good to be quieter. Living in N.Y. so long, one finds ways of moving about in a quiet way.

Sammy, I wish you well. I hope acting continues to be an adventure. I find acting to be sometimes thrilling—depending on the part.

Love to you,
Joe

42. New York, June 17, 1979

Dear Sam,

Although nothing is definite, here are the possibilities concerning our collaboration.

I could come to San Francisco around August 8 or 9 and I could stay around three weeks. The main hope would be that we could evolve a new piece—no matter the length. The last days I'm there, we could perform "Tongues" and/or the new work.

Skip LaPlante is the musician I was telling you about. He makes many of his own instruments. He's gifted and nice to work with. At the same time his work with theatre is sometimes off the wall. In other words, it works much better when his musical inventiveness is directed, so it will relate to the material in a more focused way. I called him up. He would like to come out and is available around last week of August. I have to get back to him to confirm or change.

Next thing is that André Serban is very interested in directing a program of two pieces by you, performed by me. I have always felt double responses to his productions, but recently I saw the *Happy Days* he did at the Public Theatre. It was faithful to the play, without directorial imposition. It was excellent. If it's a good idea that there be a director at all, he might be a good choice. It's hard for me, as an actor, to take direction from anyone I don't have a high regard for. So far, André is the only American director I feel interested in working with.

It's possible that Papp would put this program on. He has told me that if I find anything I want to perform in, he would do it. . . . There is no better situation in New York. Only maybe Ellen Stewart.

Now, we also don't have to follow any of these things—that is Skip as musician, André, Papp. I have no stakes in that particular structure.

Professionally, there are very few things I want to do. Most of all I would like to perform now. I don't know in what context. With you there's a possibility of a focused, strong piece. If not, there's "Tongues" already, which I think is a wonderful piece. Performing has an immediate interest for me. I want to find rhythms, expressions, ways of using voice, of speaking with words and with the face and eyes and breathing. I'm always trying things through other actors and I have a strong interest to do it out of myself. I don't mean that this is a final direction. I try to follow an intuition in making choices professionally, because it's so confusing how to proceed. There isn't any clear right direction and so few circumstances remaining which are potentially creative. . . .

I don't mind coming out there. I'm looking forward to our working together. I would like to stay in that hotel I was in before, with all the old people. It was convenient, moderately priced, and with a nice view.

In terms of auxiliary things, if there is a circumstance, I would be glad to talk to a group somewhere—once only.

If there is foundation money available, I would be glad for anything that would help pay transportation and living expenses.

Let me know how this seems. I haven't thought out anything very carefully and am open to replanning. The only part that is mostly inflexible is the period of time, but even that might possibly be able to change, if that doesn't suit your time.

I'll be involving ArtServices to help make arrangements once I hear from you.

Wishing you all good.

Love,

J.

43. New York, June 23, 1979

Sammy,

Here is an idea which occurred to me as something that might interest you and which interests me, but not in this way. I ask you to please think of it with the same distance that you regard an idea or image that comes up, which you can as easily dispose of, as you could consider or develop or transpose.

one or two people during a
    series of movements
(the words and sounds being articulated
    while the movement series continues)
The movement might be a kind of fake yoga
    or   not fake yoga
    or   ordinary morning exercise
    or   invented movements
The attention of the spectator, as of
    the actor, is split attention.
Sometimes different thoughts in different postures
Sometimes thoughts invading
    spoken or sung
Sometimes a previous thought returns
other times brought up once
to look at
to see and feel
    disparate signals and themes
One voice could be about the body alone
One could be about love affairs and
    abandonment
Transitional voices of other, even mythic
    characters returning to

an essentailly comic voice observing
  and commenting on changes
maybe about feelings

In terms of context, it's so hard to know what to do. There isn't any existing one that is fertile.

Papp wants to do something that comes from you and me. If it's a full program, he wants to do it one way. If it's short, he may not be interested. I would like to perform. I don't care whether it's with him or otherwise. And I know that neither of us has any interest in making a "full program" to round out an evening. At least that is not an aim.

In terms of directing anything, it would be best if you were to do it. If there is a way, I think that would be best. If not, maybe André S. or maybe no one.

Let me know your thoughts.

Love,

J

44. New York, June 25, 1979

Dear Sam,

The reason I had suggested performing "Tongues" in S.F. was that we wouldn't feel too much pressure to perform the work that is developed in August, and assuming something has to be performed in order for there to be any support.

It would be preferable to do a new work if it goes that way. It seems fine to me that you not perform this time. It would also free you more to make some judgments about the music, staging, etc.

The first thing that's coming up is that Skip wants to know when he should plan to come. It's a matter of guessing. So far, I suggested that he come the last ten days or so of August.

As for money for expenses, I can get a limited amount by calling this part of the Winter Project. That could pay either mine or Skip's expenses. If you have a way through the theatre of covering other expenses, it would help. Don't go to any trouble, because that can be worked out one way or another.

Skip is eager to do it and wants also to get some feedback from you on the possible ways that he could do the music for "Tongues," so in the fall or winter, he and I could perform "Tongues" in New York. He's a very flexible musician who mainly plays percussion but also invents some homemade instruments.

I haven't written to Ronnie Gilbert. I don't know what her schedule is. I don't know if you would prefer to have a second actor or not. If you want additional musicians to be part of this August collaboration, that's fine with me. Then whatever we do in S.F., Skip could teach people in N.Y., so it could be done here.

Wishing you well,

J.

---

45. *New York, June 29, 1979*

Sam,

I'm very glad about our starting point so far, as you describe it.

Any arrangements, things, and all details should be sent to Jane Yockel, ArtServices. . . .

Also, it's fine with me to delay all those considerations of where and how it would be performed, until we are in focus more—once this piece is developed.

I'll keep writing to you.

Love,

J.

What about one part/voice/section or something being about love and romance or being left and turned away from, as a wandering-off voice.

---

46. *New York, July 3, 1979*

Dear Sam,

It's a relief to know that we won't have to perform the new work, even though that may be the very thing we would want to do once we saw the direction it was taking.

Skip is away for July. I will leave a message for him that he should come as early as he is available in August. I can't remember what his schedule is. During July he's in the woods without communication. I think it would be a good idea if he came earlier, too. Partly I was going by a memory of "Tongues" and partly I was trying to be careful of the budget. Before he left, he said this project had priority for him.

I'm very glad you'd like to bring in another musician. Bringing in melody and tones can only be valuable as a dimension to include.

Since you don't have a strong preference about Ronnie, I would like to think about it a little longer. At this point my thought would be to go as we are.

Be well.

love,

J.

47. *New York, July 7, 1979*

Sam,

One thought is that it's one side of a dialogue. The other side is not there—is silent. During the silences there would be listening and even gesturing, as though to the other lover speaking.

Another thought is to have another actor in dialogue. Two people I thought of are Priscilla Smith or Joan Macintosh. They're both excellent. I don't know what their schedule is like, or if you want to go in that direction. I can find out, if you let me know.

Another idea is that there are two main voices and I do both. . . .

48. *New York, July 11, 1979*

Dear Sam,

Tried calling you. Will try again.

My problem is that if "Tongues" goes from Sept. 5 through 10, that gets late for me. Is it possible that "Tongues" could be done much earlier, like August 25 or 26? It will be easy to do with Skip, and we can continue working on the new piece at the same time.

If that can't be moved, I might have to come out there a little later, since I can't be gone for much more than three weeks from New York.

Where I stay: if there is a sublet anyone knows about. Otherwise some hotel, like the old people's home from last time. It was quiet and moderately priced with a nice view, but it was a little depressing sometimes. Not much. Mainly I guess I need to stay in a convenient place, since I get lost easy and don't drive. Also, somewhere I can make a little noise while trying things out.

If there is any problem with that, I can contact a few people I know in S.F. and see what they know about.

I'm unclear whether John Lion is involved with our project this time, or not.

Love,

49. [New York, July 1979]

Sam,

Apart from the logistical and structural questions, which will be worked out, I hope, things come into my mind about this piece. I don't know what to do with it. If you have any beginning images, words, that you want me to become familiar with, send them. It's clear that we could go the other direction—not to write each other about the piece and to begin when we meet in August. Also, if you want me to read something or hear particular music or singing or voice.

I'll be bringing a cassette player with cassettes.

Lately I've been reading a lot, which I do, it seems, in the summer. From different times and cultures.

Is it a dialogue in which only one is heard? Shall I think of a particular group of people and how they agree to talk to one another?

I've had different images of the body and expression of face speaking and even some broken lines and severed phrases, but I don't know which to follow or make or something else.

I read first interviews with Sartre in a new book *Life/Situations*. He can't write now—only talk. I read Virginia Woolf's memoirs;

Orage on different things. I've been involved in movements to bring the boat people, who are little by little drowning in mid-water, to a refugee landing in America.

A woman I don't know from Missouri wrote her dissertation on the French philosopher Merleau-Ponty and me. It's very good, even though it's scholarly writing. If that or anything else that you might not be able to get there, would interest you, I'll send it [Hendrix, Erlene Laney. "The Presence of the Actor as Kinetic Melody: A Study of Joseph Chaikin's Open Theatre Through the Philosophy of Maurice Merleau-Ponty." Diss. Univ. of Missouri-Columbia, 1977.].

About the other matters:

1. What financial things will be covered through the San Francisco theatre? tickets, accommodations, etc. If I know what's not covered, I could work on that here.
2. Shall I contact various people in S.F. about possible sublet or is it easier to stay at the hotel?
3. What shall I tell Skip about his arrangements? I understand that we play at the Eureka from the 6th through the 11th—probably the new piece—maybe "Tongues" instead. Maybe both.

I will let you know next week when I'll be arriving, now that the schedule has changed and I need to shift things around here.

It strikes me that anything to do with love has somewhere along the line to do with battle.

Apart from my eagerness to work on the coming piece, I look forward to seeing you, O-Lan and old Jess very much.

Love,

J.

50. Mill Valley, California, July 18, 1979 [*unfinished letter, not sent*]

Dear Joe,

Here's just a few random thoughts about situations that might be interesting to explore.

—How the lover is reminded of himself in the one he loves. In other words, something draws him to the other because he recognizes a familiar world.

—How the lover hopes for liberation through the other.

—How the longing for another might be related to the longing for another life. A life beyond the ordinary.

—Falling in love with different aspects, like the voice, a movement, an attitude, the eyes.

51. *New York, July 22, 1979*

Dear Sam,

I've sent you the dissertation about Merleau-Ponty and me. Since you know me, I think what would be most interesting is for you to look at Merleau-Ponty's quotes. He's amazing.

I went through phrases I wrote and in looking at them a second time, I think there is nothing worth sending.

BUT

I remembered Kafka and am sending you some of his things. I imagine you're familiar with most of it and even *Metamorphosis*. It just struck me today, it's also possible to speak out of the mouth of a non-human creature. A different perspective is possible.

In a few days the scheduling thing ought to be straightened out. I'm sorry not to have kept the different factors in mind before Skip took off.

Love,

J.

52. *New York, July 22, 1979*

Beside the Kafka stories, I'm also sending a book by Simone de Beauvoir. The last pages are about death. The rest of the book is written from a special moment in Europe and the world. Maybe it will interest you.

Also a book called *Geography of Poets*—on p. 323 is a poem by

James Dickey "Sheep Child." Another form of non-human speaking a story.

with love

J.

53. *Toronto, July 23, 1979*

Dear Sam,

I'm on an airplane which goes to Toronto. The people at the airport seemed nervous. *Time* magazine had something like "changing times" on the cover.

People in New York look happier than usual. As though they are enjoying living. I am too, mostly. There is such a feeling of immanence.

I don't know if you got my letter about the book, *The Informed Heart*, by Bruno Bettelheim. The first one hundred pages is theoretical, psychological premises. It later becomes a description of people together in some of the most extreme conditions of living imaginable. For that reason it is very hard to take. But it feels to me that it has value to read now. It was Grotowski who put it into my hand.

I wonder if there are things that everyone has in common. What would a list be?

When I think about your idea to do with gesture, body, face expression, in relation to, disagreement, harmony, and different ways—to the words, I realize I can't take it anywhere or practice and develop anything until we are together. I'm very enthusiastic about that, without knowing how it will appear.

Writing with this particular pen makes me feel formal.

I heard and talked to a cellist the other day. It was so beautiful. I wonder if Jesse is still into it. Maybe we'll get a chance to talk to each other.

I can't remember if you ever read Kierkegaard's *Either/Or*, the first book especially. That's the last reference I'll be making of books, except for Nietzsche's *The Will to Power*, especially the part about Christianity. If you have a chance and are interested, you can easily pick these up.

So much for this letter.
Best, good

love

J.

[separate sheet American Airlines stationery]
Some of the hardest things to find a way to play
are tenderness
    mourning

    Among others

54. Toronto, July 24, 1979

Dear Sam,

Although I've sent you different literature and ideas, I wish you
to know that nothing is more immediately appealing as the love
area—the lost love you suggested—the voices of love (maybe a love
that never happened, but is part of the ones that happen). And
signs—the relative connections between gesture and speaking while
attempting different kinds of expression with music is compelling
to me. I look forward to trying these.

These two things.

Love,

J.

55. New York, August 1, 1979

Sam,

Do you know the blues singing of John Lee Hooker? If not, I'll
bring a cassette of his to S.F. when I come.

It seems that the scheduling thing with Skip will be no problem—
only that he will not arrive until later—I think it will be fine.

If you haven't been able to get *The Informed Heart*, let me know.
It has no direct relevance, but it's a valuable account.

The more I consider our project, the less it has to do with books and such, if it's about love and voices coming out of that dimension and passion.

Suddenly all these people I know here want to come to S.F. I'm discouraging most of them.

Love,

Joe

56. Mill Valley, California, August 2, 1979

Dear Joe,

Something just passed through me while I was reading this dissertation about you and Ponty (which I find interesting but am unable to latch onto the terminology).

Last time we worked we met in different places, and I have a feeling that somehow affected the conception of the piece. I would like to try this time working, each time we meet, in the same place—whatever that place turns out to be. I don't know if you have any feelings about this or not. There may be a different quality of focusing on something if we return to the same place each day. What do you think? Of course, everything depends on what the place is.

I've found a woman who will assist us on production problems and generally be on hand to take care of props, etc., that might come up. She's really good and not intrusive at all.

I talked to Skip on the phone and we discussed the types of instruments he should bring. The other musician, Harry, will be working mainly with wind instruments (wood flutes), so I told Skip to bring things that would balance with that kind of feel. He mentioned glass, which has a nice range of mystery to it—from very light tinkling noises to almost violent.

Something else I thought of—what if there was a reoccurring series of phrases throughout the piece that returned to trying to reach a lost love—something or someone not present, maybe never present but only wished for. A longing of some kind that usurps all the others. Also, what about occasionally using just the music accompanied by gestures without the voice? Something that echoes what's come just before, then merges back into the voice.

I know this sounds like a structural consideration, but it might help lead us into a form that would guide the movement and shifts of feeling.

Thanks for all the books. I'm poring through the poets now.

Love,
Sam

(P.S. I'm going down to L.A. for a week—be back by the 10th of Aug.)

57. *Toronto, August 2, 1979*

Dear Sam,

I hope you'll go along with me, if I ramble now.

Again I'm on a plane to Toronto for this last trip, where I'm teaching Shakespeare and the Greeks—mainly to earn a living—that frees me, to some extent, from concerning too much about it the rest of the time.

The thing that most comes back to me from a recent interview with Sartre on his seventieth birthday (I always am interested in how people live in the world, what particular way of managing with the struggles) is when he writes and talks about "transparency." It seems to me that there's something valuable about thinking of ways and times where one is, or can be, "transparent."

I saw Peter's movie [Peter Brook, *Travels with Remarkable Men*] last night. He's in New York, just before it opens, to promote the film.

Time magazine's cover *this* week says "What next."

The thing about love is an area which I know less and less about all the time. I know it's basic.

Two people I want to bring up. Mary Brecht and Beverly Emmons.

For many years in the theatre I wondered if I'd meet a lighting, set, or costume person. Occasionally (two or at most three times) I met any one of any of those. So usually I did it myself together with a lot of help. Now I know one of each of those who are exceptional. A pure coincidence is that both the lighting person, Beverly Emmons, and Mary Brecht, who works on costumes, might be in San Francisco during the last days of our work together. If they are, they said they would like to work on the piece. If that's possible, I think that would be an advantage and a good thing.

The airline people are not as ingratiating as they used to be. In Toronto people are very polite. It's a lubricant between one thing and another. Nice change from N.Y., but I don't know what it would be like all the time.

Good day   good week

Love,

J.

58. New York, August 8, 1979

Dear Sam,

Of the two things you brought up:

I feel very open and interested in the music themes returning in some independent way. Physical gestures, words, and music moving between, in the different ways that are found, around the imagination and longings and remembrances of love is a good undiscovered starting point.

Let's work in the same place each time—it will also be much easier for the music person. Only which place? And once or twice it might be good to go outside and work. It's probable that it will be different outside in some way.

Love,

J.

59. New York, August 12, 1979

Sammy,

In the new piece, give one passing consideration to my being disguised or masked.

See you soon.

Love,

J.

[September 5–9, 1979, performances of "Tongues" and "Savage/Love" at the Magic Theatre, San Francisco.]

60. New York, September 25, 1979

Sammy,

You were clear in your letter about the names of the two pieces. I will pass it along and try to get the thing sent to you before anything is final.

I'm not sure what the situation at the Public Theatre is. I think it's a twenty-four-performance thing without critics. I hope it is that. New York critics are almost useless, except as publicity.

Hope your days are full.

love,

J.

61. [New York, October 1979]

Sam,

A suggestion about titles: the program be called *Tongues* and publicized under the one name. Then the paper program name the two pieces separately. It feels to me that "Speaking in Tongues," to some extent, applies to both—even though they go in such different directions and "Savage/Love" would still be the name of the new piece. If you agree with this, tell Woody or me.

Wishing you well

love,

Joe

62. New York, October 14, 1979

Dear Sam,

I was also surprised that Papp was calling it a workshop production. I sent him a note and said that I thought the program, "Tongues" and "Savage/Love," was of value and I didn't understand what he was intending with it. I told him further that at this point I would be glad to play it for an indeterminate period (but I really don't know what that would feel like). Later he and I talked and he said that he was very excited about doing it there and "let's see . . ." So I think he wants to see if it's too far out, or too short or something, before he decides to make it into a whole production. Also, he explained that he was about to receive your new play and wanted to see. I'm not sure what he's weighing. He hadn't read "Savage/Love" yet, but was just about to. I know that he feels that I'm an extreme eccentric and maybe the production will be in the nude or something.

If you talk to him again, let him know that you regard it, and I think he will maybe look at it differently. Meanwhile, we're about to start. I keep trying to simplify from the point of view of the physical production. The Shakespeare Festival wants Santo Loquasto to do the sets. I'm trying to get them to just work with the carpenter from the place. It's a little like a machine there, even though it is probably the best place right now to do anything. And Papp is . . . probably the best person to help such a production happen.

I'll let you know about any major things.

Please let me know how Scarlett [Shepard's mother-in-law] is.

Love,

Joe

63. New York, November 15, 1979

Dear Sam,

The "opening" of "Tongues" and "Savage/Love" is split between Monday and Wednesday. Critics are coming both days and Papp is asking them to hold off reviews until Friday.

It feels to me that the richness and complexity of the pieces are there, and also the production completeness. The audiences have been very responsive, for the most part (matinees are less vocal, for some reason). The lighting, costume, etc. (there was a kind of set for a few days, which I recommended dismantling), are very good and caring and simple.

For a while I had a problem with Skip, especially in "Tongues." Mainly that he was arbitrary in choices and not very sensitive to intentions. I think it's better now.

Papp saw it and said he liked it very much. . . .

Tonight is the last workday, following a number, with no days off. I can't sleep and now it's 3:30 A.M. I feel good about these pieces. I feel it's a good sharing with the audiences.

At this point we'll be stopping performing around the 24th of Nov. Papp promised that room to a different production, and it is the only suitable room at that theatre for *Tongues*. The other spaces would require amplified sound. For this program I'm altogether opposed to a microphone.

That's the news for now.

Woody explained that you were trying to bring Scarlett home. I hope that works out. We all here, who know her, think and talk about her with constant wish for her recovery and the easing for the rest of you that are carrying concern.

I hope you are well, my friend. My love to you,

Joe

64. Mill Valley, California, November 20, 1979

Dear Joe,

I'm glad to hear the two pieces went well in the new environment. I was a little afraid they might get swamped in those surroundings, but it sounds like you took the performance even further. I realize now that it must be satisfying for you to play them for a more extended period than we had out here and that many new ideas must be presenting themselves.

I read some of the reviews, none of which seemed to touch on the actual territory we were exploring. They all seemed to address themselves to the form of the pieces, which is slightly disappointing.

It's very beautiful weather here now. Cold, crisp starry nights and bright days with all the leaves changing colors. I don't know if you know what a poplar tree looks like, but it's always been a kind of sign to me of the high mountain country. This time of year they turn completely golden and shower their leaves over everything.

Scarlett is doing very well, considering the trauma she's undergone. She's having to relearn everything from the ground up. Walking, speech, sight, all her muscle controls. It's quite amazing for all of us. Having her at home seems to be a big help. She's going through what they call "aphasia," which is a kind of gap in language comprehension. In other words, she may recognize an object but not be able to name it or call it another name. I think you described going through something like this in one of your stays in the hospital. Her emotions are like a little child, and she goes in and out of a wide range of feelings in a very short time.

I'm glad you're taking the two pieces to Italy. It's one of my favorite countries. My first taste of Europe. Hope everything goes well for you there.

Much love and warm wishes,
Sam

65. *New York, December 8, 1979*

Dear Sammy,

Every night but Tuesday I'm performing the two pieces and mostly I'm enjoying it very much. I'm not familiar enough with the actor's repetition to know how long it will sustain, but for now it still feels very eventful each night.

This last *NY Times* article is both disappointing and full of appreciation. What most bothers me is the interpretation that *Tongues* had to do with my heart surgery, which cues the audience that it has not to do with mortality (together with other contradictory voices), but to do with some autobiographical situation of mine. My impression is that the publicity person . . . advises journalists and they think he's correct and it doesn't occur that he is just stupid.

The other night I saw your sister at the theatre. It was good to see her. And to hear further about Scarlett's recovery and to send regards through her.

There are so many invitations now for *Tongues* in Canada, Europe, Northwest America, and more and more. I'm not sure what we'll do. Harry seems relieved to be in N.Y. and wants further employment. Skip, the same, less. I feel somewhat responsible to the others and very uncertain how to choose. I'm enjoying playing in it, but I don't want to do it in a long run. I've agreed to eight weeks with Papp, and probably we'll do it more after that in Europe and maybe Canada for a few days here or there. That's probably going to continue until April. Then I'll start something with the Summer Project—used to be called Winter Project—a few weeks of meeting together with a full group of people trying out things to do with perception and things. That will go through July.

Since I read this last piece in the *Times* by Mel Gussow, I've decided to privately write to Gussow and am sending you a copy of my letter to him.

Wishing you replenishment, warm times, creative days and

love,

J.

66. [*New York-Paris, March 1980*]

Dear Sammy,

I'm enroute between N.Y. and Paris. Since *Tongues* stopped in N.Y., I've been engaged with the flu, with my love life and that diversity, and the actual living situations which have come up.

Glad for the chance to perform *Tongues* in Europe. It's my request that this or any other tour be under four weeks, because it's so hard to be away for long. The interest in the piece is considerable and the tour could otherwise go on and on.

One day maybe you and I could talk about the possibilities of the spirit. While you have gone into a real investigation, I've taken a full negative response. For me the energy or that negativity comes from a wish of some kind.

One day I hope we will collaborate again. I still think Joan Macintosh would be a good other person. But what's the subject? Or where to put attention in these scattered times?

I hope Scarlett is getting better and better. It was a strong experience to talk to her that New Year's Day.

These days I'm trying to be more direct to people. In so doing, a number of people are surprised by the warm feelings I have for them. It makes me aware of how inexpressive I generally am. Something I want to change.

My best wishes to you and O-Lan and Jesse. And to John and Scarlett.

I'll think of you while performing and dedicate moments to you as they happen.

Enjoy the spring.

love,

J.

67. *New York, August 15, 1980*

Dear Sammy,

It was good to hear your voice and to hear about your trip to Wyoming. I'm trying to picture Jesse at this time of his life. I can't do it, but I care very much about him.

Tonight I saw the Peking Opera. It's a theatre form which I've heard about for more than two decades. It was wonderful—not for thought or nuance, but for virtuosity and spectacle.

I've sent to you a dissertation by Erlene Hendrix. I know that I've talked and possibly shown it to you before, but I want you to have this copy, because it is the most careful and *precise* expression of many ideas I've had about the theatre—through the likeness of the philosopher Merleau-Ponty.

Did you receive the Bach piano-violin sonatas? Did you enjoy them? I hoped especially you would enjoy the peaceful ones, but I don't know your musical responses in the classic forms (sounds). . . .

Glad to know "Tongues" and "Savage/Love" will be published. Glad also to be doing it again. If, as is planned, Shirley Clarke directs it for a video audience, I will stop performing it. I hope it works out. Seems promising. Her interest is genuine. After a performance in N.Y., she came backstage and said, "This piece would be wonderful in pictures and for another audience, and I would like to do it."

Apart from your eye on both productions, it would be wonderful to perform together in *Tongues*. I'm hoping that the circumstances work out for you to do it.

I'm exhausted tonight. New York is humid and very hot with poisonous air, but as autumn comes, it clears up and is invigorating.

I wish you could have seen *Tourists and Refugees*. It lacked a lot, but it achieved some images which I have been hoping to do for some time. . . .

Hope you enjoy this time. Best to your family.

Love,

J.

68. *Mill Valley, California, August 19, 1980*

Dear Joe,

Thanks for your letter. It's always good to hear from you. I received the dissertation you mentioned and the great music. I couldn't make it through the essay, although I found some of the ideas interesting; it seemed as though she was stretching certain relationships between your work and Ponty's for the sake of validating her own point of view.

Jesse's got a paper route now and he takes great pride in having his own job and earning his own money. He delivers fifty papers six days a week. He's also playing the alto saxophone. O-Lan's teaching him. He's getting to be a real big kid now. Almost as tall as O-Lan.

I sent the script of "Savage/Love" to the publisher (Bantam) and, like I told you on the phone, it's only the words—no stage directions or musical indications. I suggested to LuAnn Walther at Bantam that maybe you'd be interested in writing a kind of introduction to "Savage/Love"—production note of some kind indicating how we arrived at certain choices. I think it would be helpful for those who may have never seen you perform it. "Tongues" I wrote out much more elaborately, trying to make notations on the music and the rhythm of voices, movements, etc. It drove me crazy because I never work after-the-fact like that— but I finished it and turned it in. Next time we work together I'd like to have a stenographer or somebody like that working on the script end of it if that's OK with you.

I'd love to see a script of the book you're working on if you feel like sending it.

Lots of love,
Sam

"Tongues"
(A Piece for Voice
and Percussion)

NOTE: This piece was first performed in 1978 at the Magic Theatre, San Francisco, for a limited run. It began from almost nothing but a desire to work together. Joe Chaikin and I agreed to meet on a regular basis over a period of about three weeks, each time changing the location—a restaurant, a beach, a park, hotel rooms, a truck—then, toward the very end, a theatre. We agreed on a piece to do with the voice. Voices. Voices traveling. Voices becoming other voices. Voices from the dead and living. Hypnotized voices. Sober voices. Working voices. Voices in anguish, etc. Sometimes we would just talk without trying to push the content into the structure of the piece. Other times the talk would be translated verbatim, written down on the spot, turned into monologue or dialogue, trance poem, or whatever. As the piece neared completion on paper, the concept of performance leaned toward some kind of musical accompaniment. I brought some percussion instruments into the theatre, and we started to jam and experiment with various possible sounds. Soon a form began to take shape. Joe sat in a straight-backed chair, facing the audience, with a Mexican blanket draped over his lap. I sat directly behind him on a low platform, my back to his, with the instruments in front of me. His position was static except for the face. The gestures of my arms, playing the different instruments, were seen as extensions of Joe's static body. The choices we made in performance were very personal and almost impossible to repeat on paper. These notes are only an indication of how we arrived at a means of collaboration. Anyone wishing to perform this piece would necessarily have to come to their own means and experiment according to their given situation. The various voices are not so much intended to be caricatures as they are attitudes or impulses, constantly shifting and sliding into each other, sometimes abruptly, sometimes slowly, seemingly out of nowhere. Likewise, the music is not intended to make comments on the voice but to support these changing impulses, to make temporary environments for the voice to live in. The choices of instrumentation can be very open, but I feel it should stay within the realm of percussion.

—Sam Shepard
September 29, 1978

SCENE: Bare stage. Black backdrop in semicircle upstage. Downstage center at the extreme edge, a straight-backed chair draped in a bright Mexican blanket (simple, traditional design). The blanket provides the only color. Directly behind the chair is a low platform raised about a foot off the stage floor, measuring about four foot square. On the platform are the various percussion instruments arranged in a semicircle, visible to the audience from the sides. The lighting is very simple, essentially white, and lit with a maximum of three instruments. Lights to black. Percussionist and speaker enter in dark. Lights up to reveal speaker sitting in chair, blanket covering his lap, white shirt with no collar. The percussionist, dressed in all black, is unseen for the moment. Speaker remains motionless. The right arm of percussionist appears to the left side of the speaker holding two maracas and in a slow, rolling motion sets a four/four hypnotic tempo. The sound is heard for a while alone and continues as the speaker begins.

SPEAKER:
He was born in the middle of a story which he had nothing to do with.
In the middle of a people.
In the middle of a people he stays.

All his fights.	(*Percussion accent within 4/4.*)
All his suffering.	(*Accent.*)
All his hope.	(*Accent.*)
Are with the people.	(*No accent, continues 4/4.*)
All his joy	(*Accent.*)
All his hate	(*Accent.*)

All his labors   (*Accent.*)
Are with the people.   (*No accent, continues 4/4.*)

All the air   (*Accent.*)
All the food   (*Accent.*)
All the trees   (*Accent.*)
All colors   (*Accent.*)
All sound   (*Accent.*)
And smell   (*Accent, continues 4/4.*)

All the dreams   (*Accent.*)
All the demons   (*Accent.*)
All the saints   (*Accent.*)
All taboos   (*Accent.*)
All rewards   (*Accent.*)
Are with the people.   (*No accent, continues.*)

The people named   (*No accent.*)
All the stones   (*Accent.*)
All the birds   (*Accent.*)
All the fish   (*Accent.*)
All the plants.   (*Sudden stop, no sound. Percussion-
                                  ist's arm is frozen straight out, hold-
                                  ing maracas through* SPEAKER's
                                  next stanza.)

He was honored.   (*Slight spasm of percussionist's wrist
He was dishonored.   after each line.*)
He was married.
He became old.
He became older.   (*Sudden drop of arm to floor with
                                  maracas. Arm disappears behind*
                                  SPEAKER.)

This night.   (*Unseen, low, tense pulsing sound of
He goes to sleep in   tapping on bongo, stretching head
   his same bed.   to achieve high and low tones.*)
This night.
He falls to sleep in
   his same way.
This night.

This dream he dreams
   he's dreaming.
This night.

A voice.   *(Continues bongo, mounting slightly.)*
A voice comes.
A voice speaks.
A voice he's never heard.

                               (Stops dead, no sound.)

SPEAKER: *(short staccato speech)*

You are entirely dead.   *(No sound throughout stanza.)*
What is unfinished is
   forever unfinished.
What happened has happened.
You are entirely gone from the
   people.

In a second he mourns   *(Low roll on bongo, unseen.)*
   for himself.
For his whole life he mourns.

In the next second   *(Roll continues, stops abruptly*
   he's entirely dead.   *on the word "next," rests.)*

In a second he mourns   *(Roll starts up again.)*
   for the others.
For all the others he mourns.

In the next second   *(Stops again on "next," rests.)*
   he's entirely dead.

In a second he forgets.   *(Roll starts again.)*
All life with the people
   he forgets.

In the next second he leaves.   *(Deep resounding boom from Doum-*
                                bak, moves into tense, pulsing 6/8
                                time, stretching skin.)

His whole body he leaves.
He leaves his whole body
    behind.

(Abrupt stop with boom on Doumbak. Silence, long rest as SPEAKER *breathes. The breathing leads him into next voice.)*

SPEAKER: *("Worker's Voice")*

    If I get this job. I hope I get this job. This other job I had I just quit.

(Left hand of percussionist, visible to SPEAKER's *right, comes crashing down with small pipe striking a cast iron object. Hand remains in place after striking.)*

You couldn't hear anybody talk. Soon as you walked into the building. You couldn't hear anybody. There was all this heat.

(Left hand of percussionist quickly disappears. Sounds of metallic rattling, pipe striking rim of tamborine, glass clinking, all unseen.)

Noise. You had to get up just before the light. Everything dark in the house. But this other job—this job I can sleep late. No noise.

(Again left hand of percussionist strikes down with pipe on SPEAKER's *right.)*

You get up in the light. You come home in the light. Not the same risks. No danger of getting your hand crushed.

(Hand quickly disappears. Sound of clacking wood and metal, unseen.)

Pay's just as good. Get the same insurance. This new job I can make something out of. I can move. Maybe work my way up a little.

> (*Again left hand appears, crashes down, strikes iron object, then quickly snatches up a small African "talking drum" with seeds inside. In quick, sweeping motion the arm holds the drum vertically, very straight, so it's visible above* SPEAKER*'s head, and freezes in that position.*)

SPEAKER: (*"New Mother's Voice"*)
Everybody tried to prepare me. They told me how to breathe. How to relax. How to think about something else.

They told me what kind of pain I'd have. How the spasms would come. How to deal with the pain. How to push. Nothing they told me was like this. I don't know whose skin this is. I touch the skin. Soft head. Is my hand the same skin. My fingers. I touch the head. Soft head. Just washed. Nothing they told me. This blood. This blood from me. Just washed. Nothing they told me was like this. Just born. My arm is his bed.

> (*Very slowly the percussionist's arm starts to describe a downward arc with the talking drum, causing the seeds inside the drum to fall from one skin to the other. The sound is very light and soft, like sand falling on dry leaves; the arm is kept straight throughout. When the arm reaches the very bottom of the arc, it fluidly reverses the action, again causing the seeds to make sound.*)

(*Arm comes down suddenly from ver-
tical position, places drum down
with a thud, arm disappears—unseen. Free tempo is set up on several
drums, voice joins, voice and percussion jam for short time, evolving
tempo of next voice, which is very
broken, stuttering, almost frantic
feel to it. As soon as voice begins to
manifest in words, the percussion
shifts emphasis, leaving gaps for the
words to appear in and exchanging
as though in conversation.*)

SPEAKER: (*calling*)

Where— Let's see— Is this— Wait— Now— Listen— Now—
No– Wait— Let's see— Is this– Is this the one? No— Just a
minute. Wait just a minute. Just let me catch my breath. Now!
No, just a minute. Just a minute more. Just wait. It'll come.
Don't— Don't try to— It's not that it's lost. Not that it won't
come back. It's just a temporary thing. Something— Something
must have— It's not that I can't hear myself. I can hear myself.
I can hear myself now! There. There it was. That was it. That
was it just then. Just then. Just came out. Just like that. How
could that be. How come it happened then and not now? *Why
not now!* Nothing to worry about. Sometimes these things just
happen. Something loses something. Temporarily. It's not
that big a deal. It's not like I'm not ever going to find my
voice again. Ever again. Nothing as final as that. It's like a
lapse. That's it. A little lapse. It's already coming back. I can
feel a certain familiarity.

(*Percussion shifts into very constant
tapping meter, under voice, almost
metronome feel.*)

Something in the tone. The patter. The turn of phrase. Before
long I'll be recognizable to all those around me. I'll be heard

in my familiar way. Even in the dark the others will know it's me. They'll call me by my name. I'll call them. They'll hear me saying their name. They'll say they know me. By my sound. Soon everything will be just like it always has been.

> (*Percussion continues tapping, fades slowly into silence. Rest, no sound. Next voice begins with no percussion.*)

SPEAKER: (*"Voice to a Blind One"*)
In front of you is a window. About chest level. It's night out. In the window, in the glass, is your reflection. There's a small table to your right. About the height of your knees. On the table is a blue cup. The same cup you just drank from. On the wall are pictures from your past. One is a photograph. You as a boy. You standing in front of a cactus. You're wearing a red plaid shirt.

> (*Soft tone of a gong, one stroke, then a very faint, high droning sound begins and builds slowly throughout speech, but never dominates* SPEAKER'*s voice.*)

The walls around you are green. The paint is old. In places the paint is peeled away. Underneath it's white. There's a bed in the corner, with a Mexican blanket. A calendar hangs on the wall by the window. A lamp made from an olive oil can. Now there's the light of an airplane passing outside the window. The night is absolutely black. The light of the plane keeps passing slowly. Blinking. Red and blue. Yellow and blue. Now it disappears. A star is blinking in its place. You can't see the moon from here. Now even the star disappears. A car goes by. Moths are plunging into the glass. Tiny bugs crawl. Electricity fades, then comes back. Everything else is still. Absolutely still. Nothing is moving now except for your breath. Your chest. The shirt on your chest. Your shirt is blue. Your glasses are black. A mosquito races around your ear. The same mosquito you're hearing.

(*The droning tone rings out into silence, rest.*)

SPEAKER: (*"Hunger Dialogue." These next two voices are made very distinct from each other in tone; for instance, sounding one voice in a high register and the other low, almost dividing the* SPEAKER's *voice in half, no percussion to open*)

Would you like to go eat? Isn't it time to eat?

I don't mind.

We don't have to. It's up to you.

Didn't we eat already?

Did we?

I thought we did.

That was before. Wasn't it?

Yes. I think so. It must've been.

Well, we don't have to.

No, I don't mind.

Only if you're hungry. Are you hungry?

I must be.

I'm not all that hungry myself.

You're not?

No, not really. I mean, I'd have something if you wanted something.

But you wouldn't eat if you were on your own?

No, I don't think so.

You'd just be eating for my sake?

Well, I'd have something with you. A little something.

Well, I don't want to force you to have something if you're
   not hungry.

I'm a little bit hungry. Not enough for a full meal.

I'm famished!

> *(Very softly, sound of wood scraper,
> constant gnawing rhythm under
> voice.)*

You are?

Absolutely. Starved! I'm so hungry I could eat a house!

Well, why didn't you say something?

Because I thought you weren't hungry.

I'm always hungry. I was just being polite.

I'm so hungry I could eat a horse!

Well then, we should eat!

Nothing I ate could satisfy this hunger I'm having right now!

Well, let's find a place then.

This hunger knows no bounds! This hunger is eating me alive
   it's so hungry!

Just hang on! We'll find something.

(Gnawing rhythm picks up tempo and volume through next passage. Both hands and arms of percussionist appear on right and left sides of SPEAKER, *playing wood scraper gourd. This motion is a large, sweeping half circle so that percussionist's arms appear to one side, disappear behind* SPEAKER, *then reappear on the other side continuously.)*

Nothing we find will satisfy it. Absolutely nothing. Whatever we find won't be enough. It will only subside. For a little while. It won't disappear. It will come back. It will be stronger when it comes back. It will devour everything in sight when it comes back. It will eat me alive when it comes back. It will be ravenous when it comes back. It will devour me whole when it comes back. It will go through all the food in the world when it comes back. It will go through all the possessions in the world when it comes back. It will go through all the sex in the world when it comes back. It will go through all the power in the world when it comes back. It will go through all the ideas in the world when it comes back. It will go through all the gods in the world when it comes back. When it comes back there'll be no stopping it when it comes back. When it comes back there'll be no appeasing it when it comes back. When it comes back there'll be nothing left but the hunger itself when it comes back. Nothing left but the hunger eating the hunger when it comes back. Nothing left but the hunger eating itself. Nothing left but the hunger.

(Abrupt stop of voice and sound, pause, sudden movement of percussionist's right arm jabbing out horizontally, holding a string of small brass prayer bells that dangle down, pause. Wrist of percussionist

*makes a downward spasm, causing
bells to jingle. Arm remains hori-
zontal, pause, again spasm of wrist
and bells jingle, voice comes.)*

SPEAKER: (*"Invocation"*)

Between the breath I'm breathing
    and the one that's coming

Something tells me now

(*Percussion—spasm of wrist, bells
jingle.*)

Between the space I'm leaving
    and the space I'm joining

The dead one tells me now

(*Percussion—wrist repeats.*)

Between the shape I'm leaving
    and the one I'm becoming

The departed tells me now

(*Percussion—wrist repeats.*)

Between the ear
    and the sound it hears

A ghost one tells me now

(*Percussion—wrist repeats.*)

Between the face I'm making
    and the face that's coming

A spirit tells me now

(*Percussion—wrist repeats.*)

Behind the voice that's speaking
    and the one that's thinking

A dead one tells me now

(*Percussionist's arm crashes directly to
floor as though suddenly released by*

*voice. Bells hit floor. Hand releases
bells and disappears behind
SPEAKER. Immediate metronome
cadence on wood block, unseen,
constant underlying tempo.*)

SPEAKER: (*"Voice from the Dead"*)
There was this moment. This moment taking place. I tried to
stop this moment. This can't happen now. I thought. This
can't be going to happen. I thought. Not now. I thought. It's
still possible to avoid it. I thought. It's not that this won't pass.
I thought. Not that I won't still be here tomorrow. I thought.
I will still be here tomorrow. I thought. It's inconceivable that
I won't be. I thought.

> (*Full stop, short silence, then tempo
> resumes.*)

There was this moment. This moment where I vanished. This
moment where the whole of me vanished. The whole of my
thoughts. Vanished. The whole of my feelings. Vanished. The
whole of my self. Vanished. The whole of what I call my self.
Vanished. The whole of my body was left.

> (*Percussion stops, pause, voice fin-
> ishes without percussion.*)

There was this moment that passed. Taking me with it.

> (*Pause. Sudden rattle of mallet stick
> in cowbell, then silence. Continu-
> ous single pulse on bongo sets in,
> broken intermittently by sudden ur-
> gent rattle of cowbell, then returns
> to single pulse on bongo under voice
> of SPEAKER.*)

SPEAKER: (*"Inquiry to Dead One"*)
   Is this you in death?
   If you are dead
   why isn't there candles?

Is it you, dead?
If you are
then why isn't there tears?

Is it you posing as dead?
Where are the mourners?
The grief?

Is this really you appearing?
Again appearing?
Are you asking me to believe it?
What are you asking?

Is this really you in death?
Not as you were?
Not as you once were?

Am I knowing you differently now?
Am I making you up?
Conjuring up this shape of you?
As I remember you once?
Putting you back together.

Is this me calling you up
or are you appearing?
Volunteering yourself?
Beckoning?
What are you asking?
Can you tell me?
Can you say that you know you're not here
in this world
in this world I'm speaking from?

                    (*Voice stops, cowbell "talks" con-*
                    stantly now building into almost
                    frantic persistence, as though trying
                    to break through to the world of the
                    voice. SPEAKER'*s voice cuts the cow-*
                    bell off as it breaks in, then per-

*cussion picks up quick, jagged
rhythm of the voice, playing off
different combinations of instruments.)*

SPEAKER: (*quick, halting rhythm*)
I— There— I. Me. Me saying "I" to myself. That was me.
Just then. That was it. Me. I speak. Me. No one else. That
was me just then. Must've been. Who else? Why should I
doubt it? Not me? Who else could it have been?

*(Stop, short pause. Percussion goes
into 4/4 stop time on cymbal, like
the big band sound of Glen Miller,
as voice sings in accompaniment.)*

SPEAKER: (*sings first verse straight*)
"From this moment on
you and me dear
only two for tea dear
from this moment on"
(*sings second verse in prolonged, exaggerated tones*)
"From this lucky day
I'll be flyin' high babe
from this moment on."

(Cymbal fades, short pause.)

SPEAKER: (*flat, monotonous tone*)
I'm writing you this today from a very great distance. Everything here is fine. I'm hoping everything there is fine with
you. I'm hoping you still miss me as much as you once did. I
know that I miss you as much as ever. I'm also hoping this
reaches you as soon as possible.
Something happened today which you might find amusing.
I know I found it amusing at the time. A dog came into the
hotel and ran around the lobby. Nobody knew what to do.
Everyone was in a stew.
Here's hoping this finds you in good health.

All my love,
        Larry

(*Sharp accent on cymbal.*)

All the best,
        Stuart

(*Sharp accent on cymbal.*)

Warm Regard,
        Mel

(*Ring on bell of cymbal.*)

Yours,
        Nat

(*Flat punch, edge of cymbal.*)

With fond wishes,
        Randy

(*Let cymbal ring out.*)

Sincerely,
        Matthew

(*Flat accent, cymbal.*)

Cordially,
        Josh

(*Bright ring, cymbal.*)

Your loving husband,
        Stanley

(*Sharp splash, cymbal.*)

Your oldest son,
        Tom

(*Sharp accent, cymbal.*)

Your faithful servant,
        Daniel Eric

(*Sharp crash, cymbal.*)

Respectfully,
        Mitchell Lewis Scott

(*Very sharp accent, cymbal.*)

Yours as always,
                    Rebecca

(*Cymbal rings out.*)

Lovingly,
                    Andrew

(*Soft, bell tone, cymbal.*)

With all my heart,
                    Jacob

(*Soft, short tone.*)

Forever,
                    Lucille

(*Loud crash, cymbal, silence. Percussion begins deep, driving 6/8 rhythm on hand drums (conga, Doumbak). Rhythm leads voice, then fades and swells back again to foreground as voice continues.*)

SPEAKER: (*pompous voice*)
It's not often, actually, that I find myself at a loss for words. But in this particular instance I was left speechless. Absolutely numb. No words could even begin to describe the impact of it.

(*Drumming gains force but remains in same tempo.*)

SPEAKER: (*public voice*)
I'm not here today to lay down the law to you people. On the contrary. I'm here so that you can openly voice your opinions. I'm here so that you can see that those opinions are not falling on deaf ears. I'm here so that we can join together in this struggle. So that we can unite. So that together we can bring

about a resolution to this problem which has haunted us for
more than a decade.

> (*Percussion abruptly fades but contin-
> ues a faint, pulsing rhythm behind
> voice.*)

SPEAKER: (*"Voice to One about to Die"*)
I don't now what to tell you exactly. I don't want to lie to you.
I don't want to just make something up. I don't really know
where you'll be going. That's the truth. I don't have any idea.
It's all right to be afraid, I guess. You don't have to be brave.
Who says you have to be brave? I just wish I knew what to
tell you. I could make something up. Should I make something
up? All right, I might as well.

> (*Percussion stops pulsing rhythm.
> Hands move quickly and snatch up
> large sleigh bells, held in both
> hands. The bells are shaken in con-
> stant arcing motion exactly the same
> as the movement with the scraping
> gourd accompanying the "Hunger
> Dialogue." Bells continue through
> next section.*)

SPEAKER:
When you die
   you go straight to Heaven or Hell.
When you die
   you disintegrate into energy.
When you die
   you're reborn into another body.
When you die
   you turn to shit.
When you die
   you travel to other planets.
When you die
   you get to start all over.

When you die
   you get marked in the book.
When you die
   you're rejoined with your ancestors.
When you die
   all your dreams will come true.
When you die
   you'll speak to the angels.
When you die
   you'll get what you deserve.
When you die
   it's absolutely final.
When you die
   you never come back.
When you die
   you die forever.
When you die
   it's the end of your life.

> (*Bells stop. Percussionist's right arm is extended vertically to the left of* SPEAKER, *holding a tambourine. Very slowly the arm describes an arc to the right side of the* SPEAKER. *As it drops, the tambourine makes a slight tinkle. Simultaneously with his left hand the percussionist softly strikes a cymbal. This action is continuous but timed so that the sound of the tambourine and cymbal occur between the lines of the* SPEAKER.)

SPEAKER: (*"Talk Song," simple voice, direct*)
   Today the wind roared through the center of town.
      Tonight I hear its voice.

(*Percussion soft.*)

Today the river lay wide open to the sun.
      Tonight I hear it speaking.

(Percussion soft.)

Today the moon remained in the sky.
  Tonight I feel it moving.

(Percussion soft.)

Today the people talked without speaking.
  Tonight I can hear what they're saying.

(Percussion soft.)

Today the tree bloomed without a word.
  Tonight I'm learning its language.

(No percussion. Arms stay frozen, silence.)

(BLACKOUT)

"Savage/Love"

NOTE: When Sam Shepard and I decided to work in close collaboration on a new theatre piece, we wrote each other and talked on the telephone between New York and California to make plans and express first thoughts. Before meeting, we decided that our piece should be about romantic love and about the closeness and distance between lovers. Our agreement at the outset was to meet for three weeks to compose the piece. At the end of the three weeks, we would perform both the new piece and "Tongues" for a public audience in San Francisco.

We both felt that we wanted the piece to be readily identifiable, not esoteric. We felt it should be made up of love moments that were as immediately familiar to most people in the audience as they were to Sam and me. Although we had known each other for many years, we had never talked about this subject. When we began to talk and work, even though we each had very different stories, we found that we shared many thoughts about the human experience of love. We talked especially about the difficulty of expressing tenderness and the dread of being replaced.

The first step was to choose the moments, and then to speak from within those moments. A "moment" could be the first instant of meeting the lover, or it could be the experience of lovers sleeping next to each other, with one a little bit awake watching the other one sleep. Unlike our approach to "Tongues," I would improvise around or inside a moment; Sam would write. We would later discuss and try things.

During the last days of our work together, Harry Mann, who played various horns, Skip LaPlante, who played homemade instruments as well as a bass fiddle, and Ruth Kreshka, a stage manager, joined us. Their presence, sounds, and responses affected and changed the final form of the piece.

As we moved toward performance, I became the actor looking for the body and gesture for each of the different movements.

We argued about the title. Sam continually defended "Savage/ Love." I found something wrong with it each time I spoke and heard it. But by the second or third public performance, I felt the power and appropriateness of these two words.

"Savage/Love": common poems and imagined moments in the spell of love.

—Joseph Chaikin
March 16, 1981

First Moment

The first moment
I saw you in the post office
You saw me
And I didn't know

The first moment
I saw you
I knew I could love you
If you could love me

You had sort of a flavor
The way you looked
And you looked at me
And I didn't know if you saw me
And there wasn't any question to ask

I was standing with some papers
I started shuffling the papers
But I didn't know what order to put them in
But I figured I wanted to do it in such a way
That it looked like I had some purpose

But I really just wanted to look at your eyes all the time

And you said
Look at me with your eyes
Look at me with your eyes

In that first moment
Your face burned into my dream
And right away I had this feeling
Maybe you're lost
Until now

Maybe I'm lost
Until now

And I thought
Maybe I'm just making this up

But your eyes
Looked like they were saying
Look at me more

I would shuffle the papers
Look at you
My breathing changed

Then I felt something dissolve
I felt there might be a danger
That anything could happen in the next moment
Maybe you would turn away from me

Or you could say
Let's go together
Forever

Listening Faces

When we sat across from each other
In the place where we met
You talked about your days by the water
    (*Face listens.*)
You talked about yourself as a child
    (*Face listens.*)
When we were lying next to each other
You told me your fear of the night
Of every night

(*Face listens.*)
You imagined moving to your ideal country
   (*Face listens.*)
You told me secrets about people in your life
Strangers
   (*Face listens.*)
You showed me their pictures
   (*Face.*)
You played me your favorite music
I couldn't hear the music in it

Tangled Up

When we're tangled up in love
Is it me you're whispering to
Or some other

When we're tangled up in sleep
Is it my leg you feel your leg against
Or is it Paul Newman's leg

When I move my eyes like this
Is it causing you to think of Marlon Brando

When we're tangled up in meeting other people
Is it me you're introducing
Or is it Warren Beatty

When I stand with my body facing in one direction
And my head in the other
Do you think of Mick Jagger

If you could only give me a few clues
I could invent the one you'd have me be

Babble (1)

I
Uh
I wanna show
Um
Some thing
S-s-s-omething
That uh
Some
Something tender
That
Comes from you
Uh
I
Can't
My words
Won't
Find
I wanna
Bring something out
That
Some
But
Uh
It doesn't fit this time

Terms of Endearment

What can I call you
Can I call you "Honey"
Or "Sweetie Pie"

Can I call you "My Treasure"
Or "Precious One"

Or can I call you "Babe"
Or maybe I could call you "Darling"
Can I call you "Darling"

I heard someone else call someone "Angel" once
Can I try "Angel"

Can I call you "Sweetheart"
Or "Sugar"

Or maybe I could call you "Love"
Just "Love"

Killing

It was in one moment
When we looked
When we saw each other
That I killed you

I saw you lying there
Unmourned

You didn't know
I didn't say I saw you dead

I saw you thinking of something else
You couldn't see
The thing I'd done to you

How I Look to You

When I sit like this
Do you see me brave

Do I make a mystery for you
When I put on a gaze

When I stretch my arms like this
Do you see me sensual

When I look relaxed
Do you believe me

When I'm acting interested in your words
Do you believe I'm completely interested

Which presentation of myself
Would make you want to touch
What would make you cross the border

Beggar

Could you give me a small part of yourself
I'm only asking for the tiniest part
Just enough to get me from here to there

Could you give me something
Anything at all
I'll accept whatever it is

Could you just put your hand on my head
Could you brush against my arm
Could you just come near enough
So I could feel as though you might be able to hold me

Could you touch me with your voice
Blow your breath in my direction

Is it all right if I look straight into your face

Could I just walk behind you for a little while
Would you let me follow you at a distance

If I had anything of value I'd gladly give it to you
If there's anything of me you want just take it

But don't think I'm this way with everybody
I almost never come to this
In fact usually it's the other way around

There's lots of people
Who would love to even have a conversation with me
Who even ask me if they can walk behind me

So don't get any ideas that I'm completely alone
Because I'm not

In fact you're the one who looks like you could use a little
    company

Where do you get off thinking you have anything to give me
    anyway

I have everything I need
And what I don't have I know where to get it
Any time I want

In the middle of the night
In the middle of the afternoon
Five o'clock in the morning

In fact I'm wasting my time right now
Just talking to you

(*Hums a capella, melody line only,
no words, "I'm in the Mood for Love."*)

Haunted

I'm haunted by your scent
When I'm talking to someone else

I'm haunted by your eyes
In the middle of brushing my teeth

I'm haunted by your hair
By your skin
When you're not around

Are you visiting me

Am I dreaming you up

Savage

YOU
Who makes me believe that we're lovers
YOU
Who lets me pretend
YOU
Who reminds me of myself
YOU
Who controls me
YOU
My accomplice
YOU
Who tells me to lie
YOU
Who is acting as though we're still in the first moment
YOU
Who leads me to believe we're forever in love
Forever in love

Acting

Now we're acting the partners in love
Now we're acting the estrangement
Now we're acting the reconciliation
Now we're acting that the reconciliation was a success
Now we're acting that our love has been deepened by the crisis
Now we're acting that we're both in endless harmony
Now we're acting that one of us has been injured
But we're not saying which one
Now one of us is acting the pain of premonition
Now we are acting the leaving
Now I see you in anguish
Now I watch you leaving
Now I feel nothing

(*Sings*): "The thrill is gone
The thrill is gone
I can see it in your eyes

I can hear it in your sighs
Feel your touch and realize
The thrill is gone"

Absence

You who are not here
You who are missing in my body
Holes in my body
Places like holes
Like bullets made
Patches of agony
Swimming
From my feet
To my hands

You who are gone
Missing from the place you lived in me
Instead of blood
Hollow veins
The groin is locked
You
The missing part of me
You
That disappeared

The Hunt

I've lost fifteen pounds for you
I've dyed my hair brown for you
I've designed a special smile for you
But I haven't met you yet

I've bought a flashy shirt for you
I've plucked my eyebrows out for you
I've covered myself in musk oil for you
I'm still hunting around for you

I've changed my walk for you
I've even changed my talk for you
I've changed my entire point of view for you
I hope we'll find each other soon

Killing

It was in a moment we were together
The murder took place
Without any weapon
It took place
Between two moments
In no time

It was in a moment
Between two thoughts
When the murder took place
Without any weapons

I wasn't sure which one of us was killed

Watching the Sleeping Lover

I wake up
Only a little ways
Out of sleep

You look like my child
Breathe
Helpless sleeper
Frightened of your dreams
Separation of sleep

I breathe with you
Breathe the same way
See how it is to be you
Sleeping

I feel like a detective
Spying
Your sleeping body

I'm not very far from sleep
Your dream changes
Your lips move
Talking to it
In words I've never heard

Then comes a longing
That I don't understand
Because it feels like it's toward you
But here you are
So I don't understand
What this longing's for

I embrace you in sleep
My arm moves with your breathing
Your breath makes my arm rise and fall

For one moment I think of the killing
Still
Frozen

I'm confused by the yearning
I want to have your dreams inside me
I want to strangle your dreams
Inside me

As the light comes through
And the night is turning into day
I want to know I'll die before you
I want to know I'll die before
We aren't lovers anymore

Salvation

Now that I'm with you I'm saved
From all grief

Now that I'm with you I'm saved
From being in parts

Now that I'm with you I'm saved
From hoping for anything else

Now that I'm with you I'm saved
From all other wanting

Babble (2)

I
Can't
Uh
What
I want
What
The
The thing of it is
I
Some
Kind
Some kind of
Something
Won't
Come
Out
The
Way
I
Uh
Nothing
Seems
To

Uh
Fit
The
Expression
That
I
Uh
Um
Want
Won't
Uh
Come

Hoax

Even though you see it's a hoax
We continue as though it isn't

Even though we're duped
We agree to continue

Opening

Sometimes I would want to reach
My arm would start
Something in my arm would start

Sometimes I would almost reach
Something near my neck would move
And then come back

I wanted something on my face to show
Some sign
Unlock my face
Instead I lock my arms

The head would nod
While you spoke
I wasn't sure about the head

Wasn't sure what it was saying
While I listened
Wasn't sure what you saw it saying
Agreeing or denying

I wanted my mouth to move
To carry something across
Some sign
One eye was going with it

Is this the face that shows me

It was a moment I wanted to be strong
Through the chest
It fell
You saw it falling
I went on as though you didn't
I brought it back

I was wanting to be clear through the hands
While the voice kept talking
I held my face together
My mouth on my hand
Then it dropped
My hands held each other

All the time you saw me

My whole body began to shudder
Everything began to shudder
Nothing would hold still

You tried to show me you didn't see me shaking

You took my hand away from me
And everything stopped

From your fingers I returned
You
You

You
You
(*Repeats.*)

(*Light fades to* BLACKOUT.)

Notes

1. Sam Shepard, *Seven Plays* (New York: Bantam, 1981), 302.

2. Cary Groner, Interview with Chaikin from a Portland, Oregon, newspaper, October 28–November 3, 1980. Chaikin clipping file, Kent State University.

3. Ibid.

4. Blumenthal, *Joseph Chaikin*, 178.

5. Joseph Chaikin, "Notes on the Character . . . And the Setup," *Performance* 1:1(1971), 81.

6. Robert Goldberg, "Sam Shepard: Off Broadway's Street Cowboy," *Rolling Stone College Papers*, Winter 1980, 44.

7. Blumenthal, 173.

8. Groner, Interview.

9. Shepard, 322.

10. Bernard Weiner, Interview, *San Francisco Chronicle*, September 3, 1979.

11. Program, "Savage/Love" and "Tongues," Eureka Theatre, San Francisco, September 5, 1979.

-- 3 --

The Workshop
in Cambridge

Shepard was increasingly involved in film acting during the years after the opening of *Tongues*. He completed location work in Texas for *Raggedy Man* in 1980. *Frances* was shot in 1981, *The Right Stuff* in 1982, and *Country* in 1983. His play *True West* opened at the Magic Theatre in July 1980. He staged his next play, *Fool for Love*, at the Magic Theatre at the beginning of 1983. By the time of the release of *The Right Stuff* in 1983, both *True West* and *Fool for Love* were enjoying successful off-Broadway productions in New York. Shepard had established his reputation as one of the United States' foremost playwrights. His film work kept him before a vast popular audience, and his performance in *The Right Stuff* received an Oscar nomination.

It was a difficult period in Shepard's personal life. His letters to Chaikin during this period reflect some of the intensity of his feelings. His affair with Jessica Lange had been much publicized. After the opening of *Fool for Love*, he separated from his wife and child and moved to Santa Fe with Lange.

Chaikin's work continued to alternate between the Winter Project workshops and specific productions. While performing *Tongues* in New York, he staged Beckett's *Endgame* at the Manhattan Theatre Club. During the first part of 1981, he developed a solo performance, *Texts*, based on Samuel Beckett's *Texts for Nothing*. It was performed at the Public Theatre in March and toured in Europe, Canada, and the United States. The Winter Project performed a second version of the 1980 work, *Tourists and Refugees*, at LaMama in June 1981. In February 1982, the Winter Project performed a piece concentrating on death and mourning, *Trespassing*. The final Winter Project production, *Lies and Secrets*, opened in March 1983 and was performed in London in May, retitled *Trio*. During the summer of 1982, Chaikin and his dramaturge, Mira Rafalowicz, collaborated on a piece, "Imagining the Other," in Israel. This work used a company made up of Arab and Israeli actors.

Chaikin, like Shepard, had entered a period of transition in his work. In the fall of 1983, he decided to discontinue the Winter Project. He was considering a variety of projects. He performed the title role in *Uncle Vanya* directed by André Serban. He accepted an offer to direct *Waiting for Godot* in Stratford, Ontario, and began studying the role of *King Lear* for a possible production at the New York Shakespeare Festival.

Finally, after three years of conflicting schedules, Chaikin and Shepard were able to plan a workshop early in 1984. The American Repertory Theatre in Cambridge, Massachusetts, offered to sponsor the work without guarantee of performance.

Chaikin and Shepard had discussed in their letters the subject of lies and lying as a possible starting point for the collaboration. Chaikin, however, had explored this topic in his last Winter Project production, and his interest seemed to shift to the idea of "questions" or an "interrogation." Chaikin also suggested as possible subjects the "captured angel" or the "idea of someone who lives in another world, trapped in this one." [Letter 84] The captured angel had been an idea developed by Will Patton in *Tourists and Refugees*. Shepard suggested the idea of "lostness" and the concept of "home," two central themes in Chaikin's own work.

When the workshop began in February 1984, a decision was made to develop the character of an alien who addresses the audience in a series of formal statements about his world and its inhabitants. Each formal presentation would use a different voice. The alien's interjections would be in his own voice. Although there were some very funny sequences and a fine monologue describing the customs for the dying, Chaikin and Shepard abandoned this material after about a week. They began work on the idea of the "captured angel." Michelle Collison George, who had worked with Peter Brook and had played the lead in Chaikin's *Electra*, was asked to perform the role of the guard and interrogator of Chaikin's angel. The innocence and poetry of the angel are contrasted with the single-minded brutishness of the guard. At one point the guard breaks down and reveals a deeper level of character in a chant. Here it seemed that the work might develop the contrast between the angel who died at birth and has, therefore, not "lived" and the pain of living expressed by the guard. This was not developed, however, and the interrogation continues as at the beginning, although it includes a long monologue by the angel describing an earlier mission on earth to seek a dead politician's soul. Chaikin and Shepard were aware that more time than had been scheduled was needed to deal with the problems they were facing with the piece. The workshop was concluded without a performance. Chaikin's manuscript ends with the note: "At this point we decided to continue with the Angel in a different context."

Chaikin had to leave Cambridge and prepare for a workshop in Israel in March. There was talk of resuming the workshop in April, but this proved impossible for Shepard, who was preparing to film *Fool for Love* in New Mexico with Robert Altman.

Letters

69. Mill Valley, California, August 19, 1981

Dear Joe,

I think it would be very exciting to work on another piece together, particularly with the added challenge of trying to act with you in it. Hopefully, we could find some institution somewhere to fund it and just set aside a short time (up to three weeks?) to accomplish it. I would prefer if we met somewhere that's not "home" for either of us. Some college maybe? Right now I'm not at all certain about when I'll be free, but if I know far enough in advance I can make time for it.

Both ideas you proposed ("lies" and the interviewer situation) appeal to me strongly, plus I know once we plunge into it, many other ideas will sprout up.

I'm still reading *Brothers Karamazov*—it's got a hold of me like a prairie fire.

Hope to hear from you soon. Any new thoughts.

(I should also tell you I'm not that crazy about videotape, but we can work that into it if it has value for you.)

Please write me your feelings.

Love,
Sam

70. Mill Valley, California, November 6, 1981

Dear Joe,

I've been traveling a lot the past few weeks. . . .

I've come across this awesome poet via Castaneda—his name is Cesar Vallejo (Peruvian). I don't know if you've ever heard of him, but if you can get this book of his called *Posthumous Poems*, translated by Clayton Eshelman—they're poems of uncanny beauty and very sad but with that kind of heart that Neruda wrote with. I'll try to send you a poem of his.

By the way, thanks for the Brecht poetry. One of my favorite lines is: "You can make a fresh start with your final breath." . . .

I do want to work with you again no matter what. It looks like the best time for me is going to be next winter (Nov.-Dec.). Someone from ArtServices wrote me about doing it at Harvard at about that time of year, which sounds fine. I'm ready for a little East Coast at this point.

I still have no clear idea about a format for us to work out of, but I'm sure that will emerge the more we agree on the territory we want to speak out of. My feeling about videotape is negative, but I wouldn't mind working with a filmmaker. Someone who wanted to work along with us from the start. Film just seems a whole lot warmer to me than video. And I don't agree with the whole attitude that because video is cheaper and available to the masses that it's necessarily important. What about Robert Frank? Do you think he'd be interested?

Please keep writing if things occur to you. I hope you're feeling healthy and strong these days. I think about you.

Love,
Sam

71. *Mill Valley, California, February 12, 1982*

Dear Joe,

. . . I think this idea about lying is great. I would like to explore that whole area—it's slightly spooky but very interesting—I don't understand it at all. Especially how the lie grows. How the part that originally knew the lie was a lie begins to forget and becomes a conspirator in the lie—becomes confused about notions of truth and false. I'm wondering how you see going about it this time. Should we set up a situation or just talk about it for a while? I'd be free to work with you probably around August, and I'd be willing to do it almost anywhere. I'd like to go back East since I haven't been there in so long. A college would be okay. Let's definitely try to put it together in some way.

This movie thing I've been doing is very new to me, and the novelty of it is beginning to wear off. But I do enjoy stepping into a completely different life like that and then stepping back out again. I also want to direct a film that I'm writing, so it's a good experience to be in the situation itself. It's also a crock of shit if you look at it closely. It's extremely vain and money-oriented, but I feel like a spy in the midst of it.

Another part about lying is *pretending*. The pretender. And even the actor himself. Anyway, it seems like there could be a flood of material that could come, and we should try it. I'll keep writing now that I'm back home.

You sound like you're feeling great.

Love,
Sam

72. *Mill Valley, California, March 18, 1982*

Dear Jane [Yockel, ArtServices],

Thanks for your letter. I'll try to give you some details on my plans, as best I can at this point: I'll be directing a play of mine at the Magic Theatre, which should be open by the first week in August. I should be able to work with Joe at that point, but I won't be involved in the Playwright's Festival this year. That means I could work with Joe at his convenience. I think it better if that exchange between us was regarded more as a preparation for something later in the year because there's not really enough time in a week to develop anything substantial.

I have no firm dates for anything in New York yet. There was a proposal to do a reading sometime in November, but I haven't agreed to it yet. I would go along with the place Joe prefers to work—Boston or N.Y.—it doesn't matter. Time-wise I would prefer late Oct.-early Nov., but that's also flexible. As far as working space goes, I would leave that up to you, but please don't worry about a place for me to stay because I'd prefer to stay alone—probably a motel or something.

I'm also looking forward to working with Joe again—so tell him we'll meet up in Aug., when he's out here and start the ball rolling.

Hopefully, by then I'll know more specifically about my time in the fall, and then we'll plan from there.

All the best,
Sam

73. *Mill Valley, California, September 8, 1982*

Joe,

I'm just not able to commit myself right now to anything. I know I want to work with you again—that's a certainty, but I just can't lay down an exact time because other things are up in the air for me. I have to direct my new play in Jan.-Feb. now because one of my actors got a film and won't be free until then. I won't go into all the boring details of my other commitments, but I just don't know when I'll be free—especially to go to N.Y. The other side of it is I haven't been with my family enough this past year because I was away on location most of the time.

I guess the only thing I can say right now is that I'll have to wait and take a chance that when some time comes up for me it will coincide with your time. I'll try to let you know well in advance.

Hope you're feeling good and please write me whenever you feel like it—even if it's not to do with our project.

Love,
Sam

74. *Mill Valley, California, November 30, 1982*

Dear Joe,

Thanks for the letter. I'm still up in the air about the future. I can't seem to even plan a day ahead of time, let alone weeks or months. I get more and more restrained about committing myself as time goes on because I can't tell what I'll be feeling like in advance. So all I can say, still, is that I don't know when we could do something together, and yet I know I would be glad to do it again sometime. I hate to sound so vague, but I don't know what else to say.

I've finished a lot of work recently—my book [*Motel Chronicles*], a long film outline, and my play. Already I want to jump into something new, but I don't know what it is yet. I still find these times of *not knowing* very exciting and also frustrating. You work completely different than me, and part of the thrill of working with you was this difference. For instance, I never start with a subject—like we did more or less on "Tongues" and "S./L." It never occurred to me before that you could begin with an actual subject and work around it like we did. It was a new kind of experience for me. The subject of "lying" interests me a lot, but right now it doesn't seem to be the approach I want to take—yet I can't say what approach I do want to take. You have to begin somewhere, of course, but I need something very personal now to get me going. I don't know if this makes sense. I have no idea of aesthetics—I'm just finding certain experiences—certain states of mind very powerful lately, and I want to find a way to explore them without naming them—almost as though they're being discovered in the moment. I realize this is a very private kind of thing and lends itself to writing by oneself and not to collaboration. I don't, in any way, want to push you away from the idea of doing something together because I think we need to go further with what we've already started. I'm just saying that right now I can't do it.

I hope everything goes good with the Winter Project and please write when you feel like it. I love hearing from you.

Your friend,
Sam

75. *Mill Valley, California, January 19, 1983*

Dear Joe,
. . . I'm in the third week of rehearsal here at the Magic for my new play called *Fool for Love*, which is really an outcome of all this tumultuous feeling I've been going through for the past year. It's a very emotional play and, in some ways, it's embarrassing for me to witness but somehow necessary at the same time. I've got some incredible actors working with me, and it feels good to direct again. I want to ask you something about this new play—after it opens

here in Feb. it's committed to the Circle Rep. in New York around mid-May, possibly the second week in May. I want to send this production out there so I don't have to worry about somebody else's version in New York—but I may not be able to get out there myself to watch over it. I was wondering if you'd be willing to oversee the actors in my absence and sort of keep things intact if I wasn't able to get there. I just don't think I can trust anyone else, so that's why I'm asking. If you have any interest in this at all, I could send you a script and see what you think.

As far as *Tooth of Crime* goes, I'd love to have you direct it but not with Papp. . . . If there's any other avenue open to you, I'd be glad to go with it.

Steve Gomer just recently came out here and shot an interview with me for your film. It was strange harking back to the early days on Spring Street, and he had some still photos of us from around 1965. We looked like little boys.

I hope everything is okay with you, Joe. I miss you sometimes. Please let me know what your feelings are about baby-sitting my play in New York.

Your friend,
Sam

76. *New York, February 14, 1983*

Dear Sammy,

The tour seems to be on. My free dates are from March 20 to May 10. If I can help your play in N.Y. within that period, I would be glad to do it. Please let me know as soon as you know, because otherwise I will make other plans.

Now in the coda of my grief from this last period of love and attachment. I have amnesia about ever having felt this way before. The feeling of loss is, for now, insurmountable. I'm stifling the wish that seasons will move faster and I will be finished. I'm pissed off with myself for a major, blind mistake of choice. Even my work has been out of focus for about a year. Something wrong to live in this half-light.

But, as you seem to be doing, I will apply to the fullest of my will to move out of this state.

In preposterous circumstances I find myself wondering if this or that person might be my lover for life.

During the last couple of years I felt open-hearted in ways I forgot. Now, like a beggar.

Reading Thomas Mann.

Be well, my friend.

Love,

J.

77. Mill Valley, California, February 18, 1983

Dear Joe,

It looks like I'm going to force myself to travel to N.Y. and work with the actors for about ten days—that would be the 1st week in May. I really hope I can see you then before you leave. I want you to see this play too. I'm very proud of the actors and find myself strangely attached to them—as though they're carriers of my emotions—I feel very protective of them. Maybe when you return from Europe you could look in on them for me if the play is still on.

These days I keep getting hit in the chest by a sadness I can't even name. It seems at times like it's much broader than a personal loss over "someone." Anything can trigger it off—but especially Vivaldi. I never really listened to his stuff before, but it carries some kind of humbling testimony—to God, I guess. The music seems to celebrate a victory where man is the loser. I know I indulge myself in these feelings and I'm always alone when they're expressed. They seem to be a dialogue between me and myself, but I'm not sure what their purpose is. I guess I dread this aloneness more than anything, but it always returns no matter who I'm with or how much I'm in love.

I'm in transition now and spring is already beginning to show itself out here. Sometimes nature makes me happy. Just to witness its persistence. I hope you're well, Joe, and your suffering gets easier to take.

Love,

Sam

78. *Santa Fe, New Mexico, August 3, 1983*

Dear Joe,

Just got your letter of July 15. It was forwarded to our new address, so that's why the delay in getting back to you. I'm still in a strange time of transition. This whole change has been full of all kinds of powerful emotions from the most violent to the most tender. I feel very exhausted from it all and at the same time exhilarated. It's as though I was swept up in a hurricane and landed in a foreign land.

I miss you whenever I get your letters and realize how much I need to work again in the way we found for our past pieces. I'm wondering if there might be a college or university somewhere between here and New York that would provide us with the time, space, and money to do another piece. I realize you can't come out here on account of your heart, and I really hate the idea of stepping a foot inside Manhattan, but there must be an alternative. I'd even go to Yale or Harvard if you want. I know the academic world is dull and pedantic, but it seems to me we could ignore all that and simply work as though we were anywhere. The important thing is to get together somehow under some kind of sponsorship. It looks like my film project in September may have fallen through, so I'll probably be free. If you have any ideas on this please let me know.

I'm glad you got to see *Fool for Love*, but I wish you could have seen the original cast. They were very special.

I'm doing a little writing now. Mostly ideas for film, which is very frustrating because I have such a strong feeling for the possibilities in that medium but also a real dread of dealing with the executives and businessmen who control it. I'm hoping someday there may be an opening for me to do the film I want without the profit concerns that make it a nightmare. I just feel that with film you can go very quickly into many different states, almost like composing a piece of music, whereas sometimes theatre seems stuck in language and the physical body of the actor. It's those very limitations which also excite me about theatre, but some-times it seems there's another kind of world that remains out of reach. I'm just going ahead and writing what comes to me with-out regard for its outcome. I just can't write another play right now.

Please write again to the address below and let me know if you have any ideas for a way to get together.

Your friend,
Sam

79. New York, September 9, 1983

Dear Sam,

Sometimes it seems that we should start with "character," but character is immediately confining. I feel confined in any definition and others seem reduced by any fixed definition (with exceptions). But who's asking and who's replying is part of the choosing of questions and replies. Still, what are questions which resonate or surprise or bring us back to human continuity and so on.

Questions on many forms—Name, Address, Soc Sec, etc.

Intimate questions

Metaphysical questions

Secrets

Fears—what brings a sense of peril

Some questions and replies have no interest except for who—Reagan is not interesting except for his function. The pope as well. They have to do with power and control. Someone might be very interesting who has left the world and lives in isolation. But that is extreme. Maybe it's more interesting to find things in the ordinary.

Something about what one does alone. Expects. Or how to assemble the preceding day or the day to come. Something to do with expecting. Life to change? or what inducement to go on.

What about the shy?

What about humor?

                         questions
or the oddness of an animal or vivid plant that doesn't "fit" with one's scheme of life! or insects.

There could be an interest in the questioner changing or the one answering changing on the basis of the questions.

Becoming something for the question or after??

Plenty of time to think about it.

Did you ever read "The Grand Inquisitor"—a section from Dostoevsky's *Brothers Karamazov*?

Interrogation. Interrogator.

Another point maybe is winning or losing on the basis of answers. People are interviewed for a job.

> *To win or lose*
> Prisoner—parole committee
> *To win or lose*
> To get into heaven
>   or not
> First thoughts

Love,
J.

[Note by Shepard on back of this letter]
Stranded in a World: (or just plain stranded)
2 "characters"—sitting—both facing and side by side
music—behind—instruments—tapes.

80. [*October 1983*]

Sam,

What if the person asking questions was some kind of angel— to a person.

Love,
J.

or the other way around

81. *Waterloo, Iowa, October 15, 1983*

Dear Joe,

Sorry, it's been awhile getting back to you. I'm here now in Iowa—your home state—although I know you don't feel much "home" attached to it. I'm sort of in the mouth of the mad-movie-machine here trying to make a film about the plight of the small American farmer. Right now I'm drinking brandy, and I started thinking about you and our upcoming rendezvous, so now I'm writing.

I feel very good about us getting a chance to do another piece but, as always, the excitement is mixed with a certain dread about not knowing what direction to take. I don't mind that at all—in fact, it might be a good part of the thrill of working in this way. I like very much the idea of *questions*, but there's something about the situation of the interview that bothers me slightly. How do we, for instance, stay away from the "comedy" format. The Second City or Elaine May-Mike Nichols, "Saturday Night Live" kind of deal. I know these are superficial considerations, but somehow they're in the same ball park, as when we started working on "Tongues" and right away Beckett came to mind. We agreed we should avoid too much similarity, and I think we found that through allowing many voices to enter and pass through you, rather than maintaining a singular character. The whole question of characters is unavoidable and maybe we should actually begin there—in the piece. Just a suggestion. A man hunting for a way to "be." Here again, I don't want to go into Pirandello, but maybe there is a *characterless* character—in other words, a kind of lost soul hunting through various attitudes and inner lives for a suitable "character"—one that not only functions in this world but one that is really "himself." I know we've touched on some of this before, but it never really got played out as a theme. I know I'm going back on myself somewhat here when I wrote you once that I prefer starting from nothing and finding something in the course of work, but maybe we do need a kind of "theme." Maybe collaboration demands some kind of thematic agreement. I don't know.

All I feel so far about it is that I'd like to work again with a musician—I don't know who or what instrument really. I'd like to work with a lighting designer in N.Y., by the name of Anne Militello—she works a lot like Johnny Dodd—designs and *operates*. I'd like you to be the central or *only* actor in a big open space—indoors. I'd like the piece to be more outward—in the sense of addressing—maybe "broader" is the right term—like a love messenger to a multitude. Does this make any sense? I'd like the predicament of the actor to grow in its urgency, maybe from the extremely private to the extremely general. It could also be broken into scenes. All this sounds very external now, but I'm just trying to make the start toward "seeing" it—in a way that allows a kind of entry into something we can both hook onto.

If you have more ideas, please write me at the address below.
I'll be here until the week before Xmas. Hope all is well with you.

Love,
Sam

82. *New York, October 21, 1983*

Dear Sammy,

Got your letter. Glad to know where to reach you in this period.

The things that were always wrong with New York are getting
worse and the great features of the city are threatened. It seems
like an industrialized Calcutta, which I've never been to. It's
unwelcoming. People are more estranged from what they do.
There are more and more beggars on the street and general
despair.

I move around and I feel open, and then I look and see so
much misery and a lot of numbness. And something closes in me.
I'm trying to practice ways of reopening, once I go blind. I find
it's possible some of the time.

I want to get out of this town more of the time. Piles of bullshit
in this capital.

When we talked on the phone, you suggested that Jessica would
be in this piece at Cambridge. Is that still a starting point?

You must have gotten my last letter by now. What interested
me, as a premise, was the activity of the audience. The thinking,
feeling changes with the questioner bringing up something, the
replier evoking a field of dimension in the response.

Let's leave it loose.

A characterless character is something I feel very drawn to. But
maybe you should follow that and write, and when we are together,
we could tune it to a performance. If it's losing, seeking, trying
on, or even a suspended non-form of a character, it might be a
terrain to follow out of one imagination, and our collaboration
could be more to do with performance questions and the kinds of
contact with the audience, etc.

I have no possessive thing about the way we work on this.

Without any interest in redoing "Tongues," the reason I hoped
that you would do the music is the way you are able to take a line

or phrase or word and extend it in percussion, so there is a speaking through rhythms as well as voice. That's a hard thing to find—where music goes from language, opening it up, or diminishing it, or abstracting it.

Your first thoughts about a changing relationship with the audience is a fine idea.

Maybe it should be set on a stage.

Maybe there should be electronic identities in voice or picture. The guy could try to become electronic.

There could be a bunch of pictures, like a lineup, and he could talk from one here or one there. Different faces, eyes, or bodies.

At some point he could be lying in his bed, afraid to get up. That could be funny.

What if all the voices were recorded, but a live, strong presence on the stage. Some of the thoughts could be about the stars.

As an actor I feel temporarily weakened and confused from the Chekhov production. At the moment, theatre seems to me an archaic form. But that same thing holds a challenge.

Disguises. I could play a movie star. People lose and find themselves in movie mythology. You have a closeup on that world. To me it's like manufactured dreams. It's play.

Someone called me from Harvard to ask what we needed in the way of equipment, space, etc. I said I didn't know yet. And would get back.

I'll be in N.Y., except for a few November days when I'll try to get away somewhere. So I'll write or call you again soon.

Love,

J.

83. New York, October 23, 1983

Sammy,

The more I think of it, the more the "messenger" who is trying to find the character sounds and feels like a good thing.

Love,

J.

84. *New York, October 25, 1983*

Thoughts floating.

Character—Part Angel (in combat?). In other words some other sphere. An invented character. Unearthly, maybe trapped in a prison. The idea of someone who lives in another world; trapped in this one—could be one of the characters.

MUSIC: Most of all I hope you will find and perform the music. There is one percussionist I know here in N.Y. if you want to talk to him as another musician.

Love,
Joe

[left margin] Some kind of ghost
[right margin] or a ghost
            a person with *amnesia*

85. *New York, October 29, 1983*

Dear Sam,

Krishnamurti has a talk thing on TV fairly regularly. The first time I thought about him was when you talked about your interest—long time ago. I'm impressed with his clarity and especially when I think of the long time and media changes that might have reduced him. I think he carries wisdom. He's against all gurus, including himself and the dead.

Since I have no way, system, ultimate truth and I am restlessly seeking, I look all the time.

About the new piece: is Jessica going to be in it? The thinking changes whether or not.

I know that I've been throwing out very diverse thoughts.

Looking forward to our meeting time together.

Until then—I'll write or call you more.

Love,
J.

[Separate sheets with letter]
What are you thinking?
Is there anything which you want that may
      never be satisfied?

What?
How would you dance
    smile
    lean on a wall
  to be fighting
    surrendering
Can you speak with your face?
Do you have any steady terror?
What sounds do you fear in this
    room
Do any sounds stop you from thinking?
Can you say what it is that you
    find funny, almost all the time?
Will you finish spelling the following
    words?
    Goo
    Wel
    Hel
    Salva
    Tong
    Fis
    Forgi
    Mos

The questioner can sometimes ask as though there is a "right" answer. Sometimes as though there isn't. Sometimes with spontaneous surprise.

The one being asked questions can occasionally not answer, but has to try.

The bodies can change for meaning, implication, or change of approach.

Rhythms can surround, punctuate, and tap out answers. *Also* to be direct impulse starting the reply.

Or to be the reply.

Some replies:
    Never.
    It is my most constant hope.
    To be abandoned.
    Living in a ditch.
    The light of the sky.
    My enemies.
    Later

Everybody wants to go home.
I can't keep broccoli down.
ILLUSIONS
Only if our bodies are close.
Just before falling asleep.

Often it is my first thought
    in the morning.
If someone sings to me.
Tenderly.
I feel my face getting flushed.
Forgive me.
A drop of light inside endlessness.

   Some replies could follow questions. Some could be separate.
Some could be repeated. Some connected.
   Each one a field of feeling—thought.
   It could be funny. The audience attention could bounce around.
   These are some sample thoughts.

A couple of times I've thought that something might come for
you that would prevent January's working together. If that is so,
please let me know the first possible hour. My very scheduled life
makes it necessary to organize time. Now I'm not with ArtServices,
it's harder.

86. Waterloo, Iowa, October 29, 1983

Joe,
   Something's been coming to me lately about this whole question
of being *lost*. It only makes sense to me in relation to an idea of
one's identity being shattered under severe personal circumstances—in a state of crisis where everything that I've previously
identified with in myself suddenly falls away. A shock state, I guess
you might call it. I don't think it makes much difference what the
shock itself is—whether it's a trauma to do with a loved one or a
physical accident or whatever—the resulting emptiness or aloneness is what interests me. Particularly to do with questions like
home? family? the identification of *others* over time? people I've

known who are now lost to me even though still alive? trying to track someone down from long ago in my past—someone I knew *then* but now have no idea who they might be. A haunted state but *not* from the dead. A living ghost hunting now in the present for a life that is always escaping. Maybe in these circumstances we could use other actors whom you could question—actors playing multiple characters. I'm not exactly sure of the exact search, only the nature of the search—on different levels. Also, the possibility of being haunted by dreams which carry over into daylight. Visited by people in my dreams. The taste of a dream still influencing my waking state. All of this, I think, should maintain a very concrete, simple presentation without verging into "surrealism" or "dreams" as theatrical techniques.

I'd be glad to do the music—I just don't know what instruments yet—maybe it could be a combination and not strictly percussion. I'd like to work with other musicians—players—maybe even in a straightforward pit orchestra format where the musicians are visible. I guess we'll have to wait on those choices until we know more where we're going with the piece.

I've contacted my friend Anne Militello about doing the lights, and Brustein has agreed to use her—if you don't mind. She works a lot like Johnny Dodd, and I'd really like to use her. Let me know if this is okay with you.

I'll write more later.

Love,
Sam

87. [*New York, early November 1983*]

Dear Sam,

To do with identity and lostness has a precise aim in this time. I feel that should be the terrain. Home for me is sometimes someone else's, care for places, and other times very abstract. Always stirring to me. Family is remote and indelibly estranged, but I like to imagine other sorts of family constellations. There's a place in N.Y. called Family Acherman Service that has a funny chart about families. I'll try to get it.

Identity, amnesia of some kind, other people as oneself, I'm very drawn to.

Glad to hear about the lighting person. Bill Utley (whose schedule I don't know) is a wonderful player of vibes. I recommend him, if the instrument interests you.

I know many actors in N.Y., and avoid actors all the time. If we can find a way to think who are the voices and bodies of the people, I will focus on actors. Also I will be glad to play in it for the Cambridge performances.

Woody wants me to ask you if the people he's working with in San Francisco could perform it later on. It's funny to talk about something which doesn't exist. I told him I'd ask you. I like him and feel OK about his theatre. He seems to be developing in ways that are impressive.

I'm writing to affirm the terrain of lostness. I don't have much to add.

Again let me say that we can work on this piece in a different way than the others. If you want to write and imagine testimonies, confusion, fractured replies, links with the living that are lost and whatever occurs, don't wait. We can try things together and I can contribute. My feeling is that you have, in a way, begun to work on a piece. . . .

Dreams are so vast and subjective that I retreat from them, but I am subject to forces and comic innuendos with dreams of mine that toss me around at whatever I sense to be my foundation. To do with lostness. It can be very strong. Sometimes a compass, and sometimes a delusion.

There was an epidemic in England after the first world war of a disease (I don't remember the name), where people kept repeating one moment—the same moment, again and again—for years. They finally found a chemical solution as the disease started to disappear for no reason any more than it started.

TV seems to be a location for people. The Bible. The past. An era of music. Other people's image. Holding on to secrets can take up a whole major effort. And private relationships to authority. Betrayal can be an identity. Numbness is prevalent. Pornography seems almost to be worshiped. Uncertainty is pervasive on so many levels.

Love,

J.

Do you see a lineup of about two people or four people?

88. *New York, December 5, 1983*

Dear Sam,

Thinking about performing/not performing—to be clear—why don't we let performing be part of it. Both of us. For one thing, I would like to try voice with your music. Whatever it leads to isn't the most important thing. It's a way of meeting and making something. We can find different ways of meeting.

If at some point either or both of us wants to replace ourselves with an actor musician, we can do that. I have no idea who's around Cambridge. They don't want to bring anyone in. Money. They don't want to spend any. The St. Louis theatre was offering a budget. I assumed the same thing at Harvard. Not very important. I will need to get living expenses from them. I hadn't thought about it.

We would have to be very selective with the people as we go along. They could stand in and we might form parts on these others, as well as try it on—do it, perform it. And we could maintain private meetings also.

Words and parts of words and voices and breathings making theatre music out of questions and .eplies. A living ghost, not from the dead, not surrealism; lostness, spheres, without theatre techniques of dream, and a concrete, simple presentation sounds to me like a good starting point.

I met Anne Militello. Glad that she'll work with lights.

Sam, different levels, actors playing multiple parts, moving in and around music gives us a good, open start.

So I think easily about this coming work.

For me it will be good to get out of N.Y. for a while. N.Y. gets, and for times stays, hysterical. It's funny, in a way, to make a meeting place somewhere in America, by chance in Boston.

All best to you.

Love,
Joe

89. Waterloo, Iowa, December 9, 1983

Dear Joe,

I've started a couple of letters to you and haven't been able to finish them, due to my schedule here—subfreezing temperatures day after day, working out in the snow and wind, twelve or fourteen hours a day. I'm exhausted but finally starting to feel a whole new territory of freedom in this form of acting, which is surprising to me. I'm not at all interested in pursuing it as some kind of career, and one of the reasons I'm reluctant to "perform" at Harvard is that that's all I've been doing for the last eight weeks and I wanted a break from it.

Your last letter sounds like a different format, though—that interests me, especially to do with music. As you know, I'm not at all accomplished on any one instrument. Percussion is what I feel most at home with, but even that is limited. Are you suggesting a score that you could speak to? Maybe we could both begin with music—there might be a way we could sit down together with a tape recorder and play with different instruments—invent rhythms, melodies, chants, etc., and then fit a theatrical structure to it. That might be a real adventure. It would almost be the reverse of what we've tried before. I've always wanted to "compose" a piece of music, but shied away from it because of my lack of technique or theory. I did do one piece in San Francisco that I recorded entirely on piano—taped it and had this girl write it down in musical notation. It worked pretty well. We could try something like that maybe.

I'm going to send this off before it becomes another unfinished letter.

I'll only be here another week (leaving Dec. 15). I'll be in L.A. about the 19th or 20th. I'll call you from there and let you know my phone, etc. . . . Looks like I'll be finished in L.A. by the end of the first week in Jan. and head straight out to Boston. I'm driving so I hope I don't hit rough weather. I can hardly wait to get to work with you on this.

I'm glad you liked Annie—she's very good at what she does—lots of ideas.

I'll talk to you when I hit L.A.

Love,
Sam

Cambridge Workshop:
First Project

Prologue

SPEAKER: (*in his own voice*) Before I left, they told me not to worry about my lack of smoothness with your language. Being smooth. They told me not to even practice my speeches. Even so, I did take a peek at some of them. "Take a peek?" That's right, isn't it? I think that's right.

They told me not to worry about how I looked. That would take care of itself, they said, as long as I adhered to a certain basic dress code, which I'm still not absolutely sure of.

They also told me my general behavior could be relaxed and candid so long as it didn't violate any social or moral taboos.

They told me, back where I come from, that they wished with all their heart for you to witness me exactly as I am—as being a true representative of our land and people.

Now, as you know, there's great concern in our country these days about the possibility or aggression from your domain. Mainly the great question of "pointing." Or "being pointed at." "What," exactly, is being pointed at "who?" And for how long? And how many of these things are actually being pointed at us and how much of it is purely imaginary? These are some of our questions. Due to the great horror of our country's past, some of us find it impossible not to imagine the worst. I myself have no idea.

Since you know absolutely nothing about our country, and I am, in fact, the very first representative to have ever been sent here in over one hundred years, I was instructed to plunge right in and not "beat around the bush."

That's right, isn't it? I think that's right. "Beat around the bush."

(*He rips open first envelope.*)

So. Anyway—

First Envelope

SPEAKER: (*reading*) A brief synopsis of our landscape: including certain fundamental details about our weather:

(*His own voice*) They told me to use a very "matter-of-fact," "scientific" tone for this. . . .

(*Reading*) Our terrain is basically divided into two very distinct environments: mountains and desert. Mountains in the north. Desert in the south. Surrounding both desert and mountains is ocean. Nothing but ocean. So, you might say, we're an island.

(*Own voice*) Although we back home don't call ourselves an island. You here would probably refer to us as an island, but back there we would never do that. It would be almost like an insult to us if you did that. Anyway, they told me I shouldn't try to interject ideas of my own. So—

(*Reading*) All our weather originates from far, far away. We're never aware of it until it's right on top of us. We have no warning systems whatsoever. Great storms invade us from the east. These storms have been known to devastate up to one third of our entire population every six to ten years. Drought is also a factor. We are, of course, an agricultural nation and totally dependent on rainfall and snow melt as the primary source of our water supply. Underground wells constitute only about one sixteenth of one per cent of our total water source since we have to dig so deep to hit water. The average depth being nine thousand feet.

(*Own voice*) Excuse me, but I think I have additional information on this.

(*He leaves table and heads for bike. He reaches bike, starts to dig in bag for another envelope when he's struck by something. He turns to audience.*)

(*His own voice*) Inside of every few minutes. You call them minutes? Inside of every short period, I find these occurrences. These phenomena. Now, for instance, I find myself in a gap. This happens to me all the time. I could be doing anything and all of a sudden I find, rolling up in me, an urge. Some kind of a sudden urge. I don't know if this happens to any of you. And before it even takes form—before it even has any direction or shape—I stop it. Out! Cancel! And in its place there's a lullaby. Just for a moment. I don't cancel it. It goes away by itself. I try to hold on to it and it just goes away. I try to bring it back but it goes away. It was nice. It was soothing. I don't know if it's anything like that for you. And now I have an overwhelming desire to flee. I want to get out of here. Out of this room. Out of this chair. Out of this world. I can even see the wall that's holding back the urge from before. But the urge is still there. And these things often come up right in the middle of my assignments. No matter how important the mission might be. And you, as a witness, might not even see them. Sometimes there's a certain wildness that comes up. To be an animal. To give up being civil. It doesn't even have a face. Sometimes, for instance, a drowning comes over me. Sometimes a sinking and then, from that—a courage. Or a word gets stuck. Some word. Like the word, "never." Back home we have this custom where the governor of a county puts a certain word up on a billboard for one week—is that what you call it—a week? And the whole county thinks about that word for a solid week. Anyway, I don't know what you people do here when you feel these things. I haven't been here that long.

(*He gets another envelope out of the bicycle bag and returns to the table, sits.*)

Social Customs of Oceanview County

SPEAKER: The name "Oceanview" may not be an exact equivalent in your language to the original, but we hope it's close enough to something recognizable. They told me to be very demonstrative with this.

(*Reading*) The practiced attitudes of entering and exiting rooms:
   The first thing they do in this county is stop for a moment in the doorway before entering and widen the eyes in order to take in the newness of the room. Like this. And, often, the first thing they talk about is the quality of light in the room before getting on to any other discussion. After this initial exchange the conversation could go anywhere. When it comes time to leave the room, they pause again in the doorway, turn

and face the room, and lower the eyes to mark a last looking.
Like this.

Another custom in Oceanview is that everyone there un-
derstands that every other one lives in a state of tremendous
perplexity. So they make a recognition of that. For instance,
they sometimes put their hand over their eyes and take it
away. Like this. In order to acknowledge this state. When any
given individual begins to disregard this state of perplexity,
he begins to become fanatical and, in most cases, this is
regarded as an early sign of insanity. Sometimes they pull out
of it. Sometimes not.

In neighboring Hollingston County, they have a very different set of customs. For instance, upon entering a room
there, they have a short dance with whoever answers the door.
These dances are completely up to the individuals involved.
Each visitor adjusts his or her dance according to the host, in
most cases.

(*His own voice*) There's this sense coming up in me now that I'm
speaking to my enemies. But now it goes away. Do you ever
have that feeling?

Sleep (A Brief Treatise)

SPEAKER: The sleeping habits of our people date back to the days
of the Great Invasions. It's thought that everyone used to
sleep for six to eight hours through the night, much the same
as you do here. But ever since the Invasions took place, the
average sleeping time has been reduced to approximately
fifteen minutes, whereupon the sleeper wakes up with a start,
not knowing for sure if he's dead or alive. Not knowing what
world he's entered or left behind. Completely baffled until he
begins to enter full participation in his daily activities. Often,
the onset of sleep is marked by a glazing over of the eyes in
the middle of conversation. The attention begins to wander
into a dream of one kind or another. Or the voice begins to
show marked signs of droning and repetition.

In one county there is a group who look forward to sleep
more than waking. They are known as "The Unfinished
Dreamers," and their whole desire is to fall asleep and rejoin
an incomplete dream in the hopes of finishing it. In various

reports from these Dreamers, it has been noted that most all of them share one thing in common and that is that their dreams are peopled by characters in a certain relationship that promises fulfillment. The characters never change but are found in a completely new setting for each dream. No matter what the setting, their yearning remains the same but is never fulfilled. Even so, the Dreamer never gives up hope that in the next dream they will reach fruition.

In another county there is a group called "The Terrified," and they are so afraid of sleep that they stay awake until they die. Their fear stems from the original nightmare of the Invasion, which enters them as soon as they close their eyes. Although they are several generations removed, they still see the Invaders' swords; the breath of their horses. They hear the screams of their victims. These people never sleep.

In general, the entire population is characterized by a very short memory. People walking down the street often don't remember which direction they were heading. In the midst of conversation they will suddenly forget the entire subject.

There is one small group, called "The Lingering," who need constant supervision due to the fact that each of them awoke one day to find that they were completely lost between their sleep and their waking states. They found no way to return to either. Completely marooned in between.

Rooms

SPEAKER: I have to bring myself back to this room. I get carried to other rooms because this room becomes other rooms. I get carried to rooms full of people. Jumping from one room to another. A moving room, transporting hundreds of people. And that's replaced by a room full of people pushing against each other and selling different animals. An unlit room full of people dancing and falling. A room full of people in beds. A room where people are holding each other through the night. People gasping. A room full of people praying. I bring myself back through the eyes. Back to this room. In this city. On this other continent. I have to hold myself here with the eyes.

A Very General Sampling of Our Nation's Sense of Humor and a Few Examples of Typical Jokes

SPEAKER: They instructed me to be very loose with this.

First of all, our people love to laugh. They laugh a lot. But in some cases our sense of humor has absolutely no correlation to your own. For instance, we have heard that you think it's funny when someone inadvertently hurts themselves. As in the case where the man slips on a banana peel. We don't think that's a bit funny. Or blatant insults to another person, like the old pie-in-the-face routine. This also leaves us cold. But most any other situation has the possibility of being funny.

There are certain faces that people make that almost everybody finds funny. For instance, squeezing the face together. Like this. Or when they swing their arms around—like this. Right away everybody laughs when you do that. One thing that our people always find funny, every time they hear it, is absentminded whistling. Like this, for example. Or, if somebody starts rushing around real fast like this. Or if somebody looks like they don't know where they're going and pretending they do. Like this.

There's one particular kind of plant that everybody finds funny. And a lot of people grow it just to get a good laugh. A kind of a shrub with red berries. Certain older dogs are considered funny. Especially if they're spotted.

Here are some typical jokes that we've selected from a broad spectrum of our land:

How do you tell the difference between one who's moving very fast and one who's standing still?
The one gets out of your view and the other one stays.

Do you wanna see the fastest smile in the world?
You wanna see it again?

What's the difference between the worst thing that can happen to you and the best?
And then everybody laughs.

There's a whole series of jokes that begin like this: "What's the difference between all the skies in the heavens and . . ."

Everybody starts laughing wildly when they hear that introduction, so usually the joke never has a chance to develop further.

And there's also many various jokes about anyone who holds power. These are often ruthless.

There's jokes about the different positions people fall asleep in.

Sex, however, is not a laughing matter in our culture.

There's furniture jokes. These are very elaborate practical jokes where carpenters build certain types of chairs just so people will look funny when they sit in them.

There's one main thing, though, that nobody jokes about and that is the Invasion.

Sometimes people pretend to be asleep and other people aren't sure if they are or not. The pretender gets a big kick out of this. (*Own voice*) "Big kick"—that's right, isn't it? I think that's right.

Spell (The Word "Glory")

SPEAKER: There's this word that keeps getting stuck in my head. I can't remember where exactly or when it first came into my head, but it's stuck there now. It's the word "glory." The thing about this word is that I can't figure out a way to use it in my life. It keeps haunting me, but I can't figure out a way to use it. I don't think we have an exact equivalent for it back home.

Prevalent Attitudes Toward the Dead and Dying and the General Recognition of the Tragic

SPEAKER: This, they told me, should be soberly delivered without the least trace of sentimentality in the voice or undue emphasis to elicit compassion in the listener.

Generally speaking, the entire population of our country acknowledges death as being an everyday part of life. Indeed, without this recognition, life is understood to be totally meaningless.

In the case of the old and infirm: when an old man is generally recognized by his family and village to be on the way out—when death has been determined to be absolutely imminent with him—the oldest son comes to his house in the morning, just as the sun is beginning to break over the hills, and brings him his favorite liquor. They embrace and then sit silently, facing each other but not necessarily looking each other in the eyes since they already know each other intimately. They sit like this for three straight hours without moving. (*Aside.*) "Hours?" Is that right? Anyway, after this initial sitting they have a meal which the son prepares. They do not speak during the meal. Once the meal is finished, the son breaks open the bottle of liquor and pours each of them a drink. They make a toast, which is usually very long and encompasses each of their lives together from the son's birth up to this moment. Then they drink. Once the drinking starts they become very relaxed and informal with each other, and they begin to plan the day, which they both know is the old man's last. They make a long list of people in the village who they will visit. Family members, friends, business acquaintances, even enemies. Once they've organized this list and finished the bottle, they begin to go on their journey around the town. At each house they enter they share drinks with the host, tell stories, jokes, anecdotes, exchange memories; sometimes they sing or play music, maybe a poem is read. This continues all through the day from house to house until dusk begins to fall. Just as the sun is going down in the east, they enter the last house, which is usually the house of an uncle or brother. Here, the old man and his son are left alone in the main room, which has nothing in it but a long wooden table. They share a last drink together and again toast each other—again including their entire lives together in the toast. They embrace and then the son climbs up on top of the table and helps his father climb up after him. A rope is hanging from a rafter in the ceiling, provided by the uncle or brother. The son places the rope around his father's neck and hangs him until he is completely dead.

Homeless

SPEAKER: One major problem has to do with the homeless. So many of our people have been driven out of their shelters after the Invasion. A few were taken in, but most have been abandoned. These abandoned ones don't survive. They lie by the sea and fall into a torpor. In a few months they're dead. And no one tends the bodies. They shun the homeless. They hate the people they're afraid of.

[Note in Chaikin's handwriting]
At this point we dropped this direction and went to the Angel.

Cambridge Workshop:
Second Project

SHE: I was informed by my colleagues that you were picked up in Nebraska. Is that true? Somewhere on the high plains? You crashed or something? No plane. No parachute. You just dropped from the sky? Now, how is that possible? Huh?

ANGEL: I am an angel.

SHE: You can't get away with that here. I mean, that doesn't hold water with us, see. We've seen all kinds of weirdness, believe me, and angels don't even fit into our scheme of things. So you can give that up.

ANGEL: I died the day I was born
And became an Angel on that day
Since then, there are no days
There is no time
I am here by mistake

SHE: Look. You don't have to try to impress me, all right? I mean this is just a temporary situation here. I'm just here for the time being—to keep tabs on you. That's all. What happens to you after that is no concern of mine. We don't even have to talk if you don't want to. I was just trying to be polite.
Have you got any friends here? Any relatives or anything? Family of any kind?

ANGEL: I'm not from here.

SHE: Where are you from?

ANGEL: A long way.

SHE: Okay, let's not get into that.

ANGEL: Turn me loose.

SHE: I can't do that. All I'm supposed to do is watch you. That's all. I'm not even supposed to feed you. Or even touch you. I'm just supposed to sit here and watch you and make sure you don't go anywhere.

ANGEL: I can't.

SHE: Where would you go if I did turn you loose?

ANGEL: Back.

SHE: How would you get there?

ANGEL: Just go.

SHE: One thing they impressed upon me very strongly, before they left me in charge here, was that I was to see to it that you didn't harm yourself in any way. Now, you're not liable to do that, are you? I mean, you're not suicidal or anything?

They also told me that I wasn't supposed to lay a finger on you. So I won't. I always follow instructions. So you don't have to worry about that. You're not afraid of me, are you?

As you may well know, we've got a little problem here, in this part of the country. I don't know what it's like up there in Nebraska, but out here we've got a few unsettled issues. You might even call it a state of siege. I imagine that's why they brought you into this. You might even be some kind of secret weapon. I don't know. Maybe a spy. Are you a spy? Maybe you know something that I don't know. If you do, you're probably better off keeping it to yourself.

ANGEL: Take me back
Where you first found me
And leave me there
I'll find my way back
From there

Take me back
Where you first found me
Put me on the place
So I can continue on

I'll find my way back
From there

SHE: I've got no idea in the world where they first found you. I'm just a bodyguard. That's all. They bring all kinds of bodies to me to watch. Some dead. Some not so dead. I just watch them. That's all I'm supposed to do. I can't help you in that regard.

Have you got any idea where you are now? Do you know this city at all? If you don't, you're probably better off right here with me. They'll eat you alive out there. Especially if you go around claiming to be an angel. You're protected here, at

least. That's one thing we know how to do. Protect the innocent.
You look pretty innocent to me. But looks are deceiving, I
guess. I mean, look at me. What do I look like to you? Do
I look innocent to you? I look pretty innocent, don't I? Well,
I can't even begin to tell you what I've done. It'd shock the
pants right off you. If you were wearing pants.

ANGEL: What have you done?

SHE: You're better off not knowing.

ANGEL: I crashed.

SHE: That's what they told me. You don't have to repeat what I
already know.

ANGEL: What do you know?

SHE: Not a whole hell of a lot. I know there's a lot of crazy people
around. You could be one of them as far as I'm concerned.
People who believe they're somebody else. People who talk to
themselves. They're all over this city. I've even got a cousin
who thinks he's controlling the moon. But he isn't. You could
be like that. A whacko. Are you a whacko?

ANGEL: I was on my way somewhere. I had a destination. I don't
know what went wrong.

SHE: You got lost?

ANGEL: Lost.

SHE: Where?

ANGEL: Out there.

SHE: How did you get lost?

ANGEL: I wasn't paying attention. A thought took me.

SHE: What thought?

ANGEL: This thought came into me. Invaded me.

SHE: What thought?

ANGEL: I thought: "Maybe I'll never get back."

SHE: Where?

ANGEL: Where I started. I thought: "Maybe I'll get stuck in
between."

SHE: So you've never been on earth before? Is that it?

ANGEL: Once.

SHE: When was that?

ANGEL: I was born here
          And died
          The day I died
          I became an angel

SHE: And that was the last you ever saw of earth?

ANGEL: The last. No—

SHE: You just took off into Heaven and that was it?

ANGEL: They took me.

SHE: Who?

ANGEL: A tribe of angels.

SHE: A tribe? They have tribes up there?

ANGEL: It's not "up."

SHE: What?

ANGEL: It's not "up."

SHE: What isn't up?

ANGEL: Where they are.

SHE: I can't follow this.

ANGEL: Pay attention.

SHE: What?

ANGEL: Listen.

SHE: Who are you anyway?

ANGEL: I'm an angel.

SHE: Oh, shut up with that!

ANGEL: You don't have to believe me.

SHE: I don't.

ANGEL: Other ones believe me.

SHE: Who?

ANGEL: Ones I depend on.

SHE: So you are a spy.

ANGEL: No. Turn me loose.

SHE: I can't turn you loose even if I wanted to and I don't want
    to, so stop asking me that.

ANGEL: Turn me loose.

SHE: I don't want to have to get rough with you.

ANGEL: You can't.

SHE: I can lose my temper.

ANGEL: You're under orders.

SHE: That's beside the point. If I lose my temper there's no orders
    in the world that can hold me.

ANGEL: What's "lose your temper"?

SHE: Lose control. To go off the deep end.

ANGEL: What's that?

SHE: Where you get very pissed off.

ANGEL: I don't understand.

SHE: Don't you ever get mad?

ANGEL: What's "mad"?

SHE: Angry?

ANGEL: I don't know what it is.

SHE: Don't they have fights in Heaven?

ANGEL: Battles.

SHE: Battles? Okay. Battles. That's like a war, right?

ANGEL: Yes. A war. There's one now. But it's not like a war.

SHE: What is it, then?

ANGEL: A battle.

SHE: What's the difference?

ANGEL: A battle is destined. A war is an accident.

SHE: So you don't lose your temper?

ANGEL: No.

SHE: You fight without getting mad?

ANGEL: Yes.

SHE: How do you do that?

ANGEL: You just do. You're supposed to, so you do.

SHE: What's the battle about?

ANGEL: It's been going on a long time.

SHE: What's it about?

ANGEL: The same thing it's always been about.

SHE: What's that?

ANGEL: I forget.

SHE: I don't understand you.

ANGEL: You're not supposed to.

SHE: What's that supposed to mean? You think you're better than
    me?

ANGEL: No.

SHE: Then how come I'm not supposed to understand you?

ANGEL: We're from two different worlds.

SHE: You're really an angel, huh?

ANGEL: I am an angel
        I died the day I was born
        And I became—

SHE: All right. Jesus. You don't have to repeat everything.

ANGEL: My language is limited.

SHE: That doesn't mean you have to repeat everything.

ANGEL: I don't have a wide choice.

SHE: Of what?

ANGEL: Your words.

SHE: Have you got your own language?

ANGEL: Yes.

SHE: What is it?

ANGEL: You wouldn't understand it.

SHE: Try me.

ANGEL: *Flogantus nowlumti foristune nobeginto.*

SHE: You're right. What did you say?

ANGEL: There's no equivalent.

SHE: That's what you said?

ANGEL: No. You don't have equal words. We have lots of languages.

SHE: And I wouldn't be able to understand any of them?

ANGEL: It depends.

SHE: On what?

ANGEL: Your soul.

SHE: I don't have a soul.

ANGEL: You're right.

SHE: How do you know that?

ANGEL: I can see you don't.

SHE: How can you see that?

ANGEL: I can see right through you.

SHE: Now wait a second.

ANGEL: I see right through your skin.

SHE: What do you see?

ANGEL: Nothing.

SHE: Just blank?

ANGEL: A heart. Lungs. Muscle. Bones. That's about it. Nothing lasting.

SHE: Are you sure about that?

ANGEL: Absolutely.

SHE: Well, I don't know why I should expect any different, after a life of solid crime.

ANGEL: What's crime?

SHE: That's when you break the law.

ANGEL: What law?

SHE: The law. Human law.

ANGEL: What law is that?

SHE: Like when you kill somebody. That's breaking the law.

ANGEL: What's "kill"?

SHE: Dead.

ANGEL: Dead?

SHE: Dead. Don't you die?

ANGEL: What is it?

SHE: You said "You died the day you were born."

ANGEL: I didn't die.

SHE: That's what you said.

ANGEL: I became an angel.

SHE: Well, what were you before you became an angel?

ANGEL: I don't know. What do you call it?

SHE: A baby.

ANGEL: A "baby."

SHE: A baby human.

ANGEL: That's what I was?

SHE: That's what you said.

ANGEL: Like you?

SHE: Yeah. But I didn't die.

ANGEL: But you will?

SHE: Yeah.

ANGEL: Then what?

SHE: I haven't got a clue.

ANGEL: You'll blow away.

SHE: How do you know?

ANGEL: There's nothing there.

SHE: Maybe if I turned you loose, we could make a deal.

ANGEL: What's a "deal"?

SHE: A little exchange.

ANGEL: Like what?

SHE: If I turned you loose, maybe you could see to it that I don't
    blow away.

ANGEL: I can't guarantee that.

SHE: Why not?

ANGEL: I don't decide that.

SHE: Who does?

ANGEL: I don't know. It comes from way far away.

SHE: There must be something that decides stuff like that.

ANGEL: There must be. But we're never sure. Like, once I was
    here before and—

SHE: You keep lying to me. Why is that?

ANGEL: Lying?

SHE: Yeah. Lying. You say you died and then you say you don't
    die. You say you were here only once and now you say you
    were here again. What's the story?

ANGEL: I lose track. Everything mingles sometimes. I shift around.
    I'm never sure anymore where I am.

SHE: That's not good. You should always be sure. I'm always sure.

ANGEL: I'm not. There was a time when I used to walk and flowers sprang up behind me. Now look, no flowers.

There was a time when the light from my eyes was so powerful it would blind the sun. Now look, no light. Nothing.

There was a time when music surrounded me on all sides. Voices. Bells. An incredible ringing. Now listen, nothing—no sound but the sound of my voice.

SHE: If I turned you loose, maybe all that would come back.

ANGEL: I doubt it.

SHE: Maybe you don't want to be turned loose.

ANGEL: Every second
    I'm weakening
    Turn me loose

SHE: What will you do for me if I turn you loose?

ANGEL: Nothing.

SHE: You're a fake angel. Let's face it. You're a powerless wimp. You can't fly. You crash to earth and you can't fly. You've got no powers of any kind. You can't speak a lick. You're totally selfish. You allow yourself to be captured. All you can do is whine and whimper.

ANGEL: Turn me loose.

SHE: Can't you take me with you? It would be so great to escape. To get the hell out of here once and for all. I can't stand it here. I've got no future here. Can't you take me with you? If I let you go would you take me with you?

If I let you go would you take away all my pain—all my suffering?

If I let you go would you seek vengeance on me? Would you send someone to do me in?

If I let you go would you comfort me? Would you give me grace?

If I let you go would you cast a curse on me?

If I let you go would you deliver me? Would you transport me?

If I let you go would you give me wings? Could you turn me into a lion? I always wanted to be a lion. With wings.

If I let you go would you at least put in a good word for me?

Or am I too far gone for that?

Have I gone too far for that?

Am I past redemption?

(*Repeat chant*)

I'll tell you what. If you agree to take me with you, maybe I'll do you a favor. A big favor. You look like a lonely kind of a guy to me. Maybe you'd like me to touch you somewhere. Just a little touch somewhere. Imagine if I touched you. Would you like that? Close your eyes and imagine I'm touching you under the armpits. Do you feel anything? Do you like it? Imagine I'm licking your armpits. Can you feel my tongue? Imagine I'm licking your toes. Sucking your little toes. Can you feel it? Imagine I'm tickling your weenie with my nipples. How does that feel? Do you feel anything? Maybe you don't feel anything. Is that it?

Do angels have feelings? Do you care about each other? Do angels betray each other? Do you care about us at all? Us on earth. Do you dance? Do you sing? Do you love? How do you know when you're in love? Do you know it like we do here? Do you think you could love me? Or are you too above me? Could you maybe love me if I dressed up? Could you love me if I made myself up? If I put on another face? If I changed my whole appearance? That happens a lot here. Change your whole appearance and all of a sudden somebody loves you. Out of the blue.

Maybe you could just hold me and rock me to sleep?

Don't you ever sleep?

I can't sleep if you're going to stay awake.

How could I sleep?

You might cut my throat in the middle of the night.

You might tear my eyes out. And then where would I be?

Maybe I should sell you. Put you up for sale. I know a guy up on Wabash Street who buys babies. Maybe I could sell you to him. I know you're not a baby, but maybe he'd have an interest in an angel. Who knows? You must be worth something. Maybe a museum would buy you. What do you think you're worth? Can you do anything? Clean houses? Walk dogs? Wash dishes? What can you do? Maybe you're worthless. Absolutely worthless. It's possible. Maybe I'm just wasting my time.

ANGEL: We don't make deals.

SHE: Who doesn't? Everybody makes deals.

ANGEL: We don't. Deals are already made. There's nothing we can do about it. We just carry them out. I was here once before—

SHE: Don't lie to me again.

ANGEL: This happened. My memory remembers it now. This happened:

I was here once before—quite awhile back. I was sent here on a mission with a small battalion. We were assigned to deliver a soul of a very great man here on earth. I forget his name now, but he was very great. Almost worshiped by the whole population. We arrived and the streets were packed with people. Throngs of people all weeping and moaning. A big regiment of soldiers on horseback led by a general riding a white stallion. Behind them was a long line of black limousines, moving very slowly. Cannons were fired. Lines of soldiers fired rifles. Flags of all nations were at half-mast. Torches burned. The family of the dead man stood around the open casket in silence as hundreds of people passed by and kissed the corpse on the lips. Some fell to their knees and kissed the ground beneath him. We went down into the middle of this and sat on the four corners of the casket—waiting for the appearance of his soul. We have certain very definite signs for that. One of them is the "skin of the breath." We wait for that to appear. We waited all day. We followed the casket to the cemetery. We waited there. Still, nothing appeared. We checked very carefully with each other to make sure we weren't making a mistake. We sat on the corpse. On the chest. One of us stood on his eyes. Another one looked in his nose. We checked in his ears. But there was no sign of a soul. Finally, they closed the casket and lowered him down. We waited all night and part of the next morning, but nothing came. Nothing even resembling a soul appeared to us. So we went back and reported our findings to the Principalities. They told us they must have been mistaken.

SHE: How could they make a mistake like that? How is it possible for them to make a mistake like that? They're supposed to know.

ANGEL: Things have been confused for some time. Ever since the battle started.

SHE: What battle?

ANGEL: It doesn't have a name.

SHE: If they could make a mistake like that, then you could easily be mistaken about me.

ANGEL: About what?

SHE: That there's nothing in me.

ANGEL: No. That's clear.

SHE: How can you be so sure when even more powerful ones than you can make mistakes?

ANGEL: They were far away. I'm very close to you.

SHE: You're a lunatic.

ANGEL: No. Lunatics are from the moon. They belong to the moon. Luna. Moon.

SHE: Now all of a sudden you know all kinds of words.

ANGEL: Some are the same.

SHE: Which ones?

ANGEL: Ancient ones.

SHE: What other ones are the same?

ANGEL: Heresy.

SHE: I have a feeling about you that you're a very wicked person.

ANGEL: I'm not a person
          Turn me loose
          Every second
          Something's changing in me
          Growing weaker
          Turn me loose
          Take me back
          To where you found me

SHE: I'm not the one who found you! What's the matter with you? I'm working for a very big organization here. A multinational organization. Don't you understand that? They're the ones to talk to. Not me.

ANGEL: Where are they?

SHE: They never show their faces.

ANGEL: How do you know them?

SHE: We have a system. Cars and buzzers. Telephones. No one ever sees them.

ANGEL: Where are they?

SHE: All over. It's a vast network. A chain.

ANGEL: Can't you ask them to turn me loose?

SHE: I'm in no position to ask. I'd lose my job.

ANGEL: I'm your job?

SHE: You're my job. That's right.

[Notes in Chaikin's handwriting]

At this point we decided to continue to develop the Angel in a different context. Look into: What God cannot do!

-- 4 --

"The War in Heaven" (Angel's Monologue)

The plan to resume work on "The War in Heaven" was altered by a catastrophe in Chaikin's life. After returning from Israel, Chaikin began work on *Waiting for Godot* at the Shakespeare Festival in Ontario. Shortly after rehearsals began, Chaikin resigned as director and returned to New York. He was extremely ill and apparently sensed that he should be near his doctors in Manhattan. Soon after his return to New York, he suffered heart failure. On May 7, he had a stroke during open-heart surgery.

Although the surgery was successful, the stroke left Chaikin severely impaired in his speech, a kind of left-hemisphere aphasia. Friends helped Chaikin manage during the most difficult period of his early recovery, and he began therapy at the Rusk Institute. Progress was excellent, and over the next six months Chaikin regained much of his ability to speak.

Shepard was familiar with aphasia, since O-Lan's mother, Scarlett Johnson Dark, had suffered a similar kind of aphasia in September 1979. He was able to visit and work with Chaikin in August 1984, early in Chaikin's recovery. He gave Chaikin some speaking exercises he had learned while working with Scarlett. He also worked with Chaikin on material from the Cambridge "War in Heaven." Passages from the earlier work were expanded and combined with notes Shepard took on their discussions together, as Chaikin tried to express his own sense of alienation through loss of language. The resulting monologue alternates passages that grow out of the poetic voice of the captured angel with passages in Chaikin's aphasic syntax (they are printed in columns on alternate sides of the page in the published text). When Chaikin performs the monologue, the two aspects are unified through his own voice, which seems to be coming from another world.

Shepard completed a revision and shaping of the text in Minnesota at the end of August. Chaikin worked on this text in September and October, reading it to friends and mastering the words. It was a very important element in the process of recovery for him. It gave him a sense of stability through work and a revived hope for the future. Late in October Shepard returned to New York to complete work on the monologue. Rick Harris produced the recording of the work in November for a January WBAI broadcast. Shepard composed and performed the musical accompaniment. Chaikin performed a staged reading of the monologue in San Diego in December 1985, directed by Steven Kent. Chaikin has continued to perform "The War in Heaven," notably in San Francisco, Toronto, Italy, Poland, and in a new staging by Robert Woodruff in Los Angeles in March 1988. Martin Esslin, who saw the San Francisco reading, has written, "I can attest to the fact that such a text does refer to an external reality, that it does movingly enshrine its authors' intentions—and that it is theatrical, of the theatre, because of its deep human reality."[1]

Letters

90. *Telegram, Los Angeles, May 10, 1984*

DEAR JOE
MY HEART IS WITH YOU I'LL TRY TO BE THERE IF YOU NEED ME JUST
LET ME KNOW TAKE STRENGTH FROM YOUR OWN BREATH I LOVE YOU
SAM

91. *Santa Fe, New Mexico, June 11, 1984*

Dear Joe,

Here's a picture of me taken up in Iowa (your home country, although I know you don't think of it that way). It was bitter cold—got down to forty below zero—so cold the feet of cattle would freeze to the ground.

It's been great talking to you on the phone. The last time sounded very much like you know where you were going—finding your way through the maze. I'm glad to hear you're getting stronger and being back home must be a big help.

Looks like I'll be able to get out to New York and see you sometime mid-August. I'll keep calling and let you know the exact time when it gets closer.

Lots of love,
Sam

92. *Minnesota* [*August 1984*]

Joe,

I'll retype our work and send the whole new script to you in the mail. I'll call you on the phone and we'll talk about any changes you want to make. I'll be back here in New York the last week of September and then we'll work again—with some music and finding ways to act it and speak it. If you want to call me in New Mexico —I'll be there by the 23rd of this month. . . .

If you want to call me before the 23rd, I'll be in Minnesota. . . . Keep working on the sound cards and practice the ones you miss. Don't worry when the speaking feels worse or further away from you because when it grows stronger—each time it comes back it gets stronger and stronger. Just like the body but slower.

It won't be long until we're together again. See you soon.

Love,
Sam

93. *Santa Fe, New Mexico* [*early September 1984*]

Dear Joe,

Here's the version of our work that I cooked up in Minnesota. As you can see, I rearranged a lot of stuff and added a few things. It seems to have a wholeness to it now and a kind of strange continuity, but I don't think we can be sure about any of it until you start speaking it and working with it. I'm sure there's more work to be done on it, but, for now, I think it's pretty clear.

I should be back in New York around the 29th or 30th—for about a week. I'll call you when I get in. I've got lots of work to do in preparation for my play, but maybe we could work at night or in the mornings—whichever is best for you.

You sounded great on the phone. Keep your spirits high. And call me if you want to say anything about the script after you read it.

Lots of love,
Sam

94. *Santa Fe, New Mexico, September 6, 1984*

Dear Joe,

Just talked to you today on the phone, and I can't understand why our script of "The War in Heaven" didn't arrive with you yet. I mailed it over a week ago. If it still hasn't come by the end of the week, please let me know and I'll send off another one.

There's a great chill in the morning air here now—the first hint of fall. I'm packing into the mountains next week with two of my horses to do some fishing for three days. It'll be great to be back in the wilderness for a while. Jessica has to go to L.A. for about four days, so I'm going off by myself. After that I'll be on the road again. More long-distance driving—which I'm not looking forward to this time. It'll be different once I hit the road, I guess. I plan to be in New York about the 29th. We'll get together then.

Mostly, I've been working on my new play. Rewriting and continuing it. It looks like it wants to be a long one this time. About twelve characters—three acts and about thirty scenes. I hope I can find the right actors for it. Maybe you can help me, once I get it started.

I've been reading a lot of Stephen Crane lately—early American writer who only lived to be twenty-eight but wrote his ass off. Left over a hundred pieces of work, including a great novel of the Civil War—*The Red Badge of Courage*. His journalism is really fascinating. Seems he placed himself right in the middle of things—unlike myself.

I'm really eager to see you again and work some more. Hope you're getting stronger each day.

Love,
Sam

"The War in Heaven"
(Angel's Monologue)

I died
the day I was born
and became an Angel
on that day

since then
there are no days
there is no time
I am here
by mistake

I'm not sure now
how it happened

I crashed
I know I crashed
in these streets
I came down

I don't know what went wrong

I was a part of something
I remember being
a member
I was moving
I had certain orders
a mission

I had a small battalion
Principalities
Dominions

I'm not sure now
how I fit
where
I fit
exactly

I know
there were those
above me
and those
below
but I'm not sure now
where I fit

                              so many things
                              now
                              so many
                              earth
                              earth
                              just a little part
                              just so much
                              so tiny
                              you can never catch
                              so many
                              air
                              sometimes
                              earth
                              so small
                              tiny
                              so much more
                              ever
                              more
                              more
                              more
                              more
                              and more
                              and dead
                              sometimes
                              even dead
                              yes
                              it's true

There was a time
when I felt I had a destination

I was moving
toward something
I thought I understood

There was an order
that was clear to me
a lawful order

Then we were invaded
all the domains were shattered
connections
were broken
we were sent
in a thousand directions

I'd be on a mission
and forget where I was going

I'd try to return
and forget where I was going

I'd try to return
and forget how to find my way
    back

I'd be lost
in between

That's how I crashed
in a moment of doubt
I crashed
to earth

                              sometimes grief
                              now
                              grieving
                              both
                              sometimes
                              it's true

sometimes it's true
it is
grief
grieving
and grief
both
changing
yes
moving
so many times
it's true
I think it's true

sometimes God
changing
sometimes nothing
sometimes no one else
sometimes nothing
sometimes only God

sometimes beginning
over
beginning
yes
it's true

Every minute I'm here
something's changing in me
something's diminishing
my power slips away

Every second I'm here
I'm weakening

Take me back
where you first found me
and leave me there

I'll find my way back
from there

Take me back

I'll perish
if I stay tied up like this
I will
I'll perish
Then you'll be without me

Turn me loose
Turn me loose

I can't live
without you imagining me
I have no life
without your thought
of me

But you can't see me
as I'm intended to be
unless I'm turned loose

Turn me loose
Turn me loose

You've kept me long enough

      air
      now
      so many things
      now
      so much
      everywhere
      so many
      earth
      sometimes God
      God
      sometimes nothing
      nothing
      don't
      don't care
      I say I'm not interested
      not interesting to me
      but then God
      again

God
everywhere
air
everything
out there
beginning
again
beginning
yes
it's true
I think it's true

more
the more
is never
never
stops
too much
more
more
more
more
and more
so nothing
ever stops
cuts
because
too much
more

extraordinary

Take me back
where you first found me

Put me on the place

I'll find my way
back
from there

Take me back

There was a time
when I used to walk
and flowers sprang up
behind me

Now look
no flowers

Take me back

There was a time
when the light from my eyes
was so powerful
it would blind the sun

Now look
no light
nothing

Take me back

There was a time
when music
surrounded me
on all sides
voices
bells
an incredible ringing

Now listen
nothing
no sound
but the sound
of my voice

Take me back

I'm hovering
above myself
looking

for a way
back in

I'm all around this body
waiting

Turn me loose

Every second
I'm weakening

Turn me loose

air
again it comes
surrounded
everywhere
it comes
more
so much more
and more
and more
and more
and air
all around
and through
is air
and earth
and air
and Venus
and sometimes Mars
even part of Mars
moving through air
there is no end
and earth
and something so small
so tiny
air

Turn me loose

I was here
once before
quite a while back

I was sent
on a mission
with a small battalion

We were assigned
to deliver a soul
of a very great man
here on earth

I forget his name now
but he was very great
almost worshiped

We arrived
the   streets   were   packed   with
    people
throngs of people
all weeping
and moaning
grieving
grief
it's true

A huge regiment
of soldiers
on horses
led by a General
riding a white stallion

A long line
of black limousines
barely moving

Cannons were fired

Rifles were fired

Flags of all nations
were flown at half-mast

Torches burned

The family of the dead man
stood around the open casket
in silence

Hundreds of people
passed by
and kissed the corpse
on the lips

Some fell to their knees
kissing the ground
beneath him

We descended
into the middle of this
and sat on the four corners
of the casket
waiting
for the appearance
of the dead man's soul

We have certain
very definite signs
that tell us

One of these signs
is "the skin of the breath"

We wait
for that to appear
it's usually the very first
to come

We waited all day

We followed the casket to the
    cemetery
we waited there for it
but nothing appeared

We checked very carefully
with each other

to make sure
we weren't making a mistake

We sat on the corpse
in different stations
one of us
on the chest
one of us
stood on his eyes
another one
on his knees

We looked inside his nose
We checked his ears
but there was absolutely no sign
of a soul

They finally closed the casket up
and lowered him down

We waited
all through the night
and part of the next morning
just in case

Nothing came
nothing even resembling a soul
appeared to us

So we all went back
and reported our findings
to the Principalities

They told us
they must have been mistaken

Extraordinary
I can tell
where God is my life
and Hell

I was dead
so many times

ten
twelve
fourteen
twenty
thirty
now forty
so many times
I've been dead
then better
dead
now better
so many times

sometimes
so much
so much more
so much

not earth
not just earth
earth is too tiny
too small

let's say
one day
one day
dead
dead
and nothing else
just dead
nothing

but maybe it's not so
maybe   something   new   starts
    there
maybe I can't think it
can't remember
maybe not human
maybe a turtle
I can't tell
maybe some wonder

extraordinary
right now
it all starts again
again
again again again
dead dead
born
so many times
again
not just earth
so many more
and more
and more
and more
yes

maybe sometimes
love
love
not everyone
just someone
love
it's great

but sometimes
hate
I hate it
I hate someone
sometimes
I hate
hate
not good
it's not so good

sometimes war
it's war
cut
we don't want them
it's like that
sometimes
war

it's true
they hate
fight
you have to look for an Angel
in the middle
in the midst of this

Turn me loose
Turn me loose now
you've kept me long enough

sometimes
sometimes you can't bring them
you can't call them down
Angels
you don't know their language
you're not speaking them
they're not there
they've gone
now
away
they've gone

Turn me loose now

I have a partner
the partner
is me
the partner
has a partner
in me

Turn me loose

sometimes soul
looking
for someone
my someone else
soul
sometimes
looking
for someone else
soul
sometimes one
looking

Can you see
someone
alone
along
looking
for soul
sometimes
can't see them
only sometimes
and some
yes
sometimes

sometimes sex
in soul
sex
in someone else
touch
between two
in each other
or out
outside
both
everywhere
every time

sometimes together
both
changing
moving
into each other
sometimes no soul
sometimes dead
can't live very much
gone
empty
soul
empty empty
soul
without a body
looking
for a body

Take me back

Every second I stay
I weaken

Take me back now
you've kept me long enough

                      sometimes sex
                      together
                      fucking
                      each other
                      one goes over
                      to the other
                      leaves
                      the other
                      then comes back
                      sometimes many
                      living
                      in one
                      in an animal
                      sometimes
                      in a bird
                      same
                      between
                      two animals
                      sometimes
                      new
                      nothing's different
                      sometimes
                      ancient
                      old old old
                      before birth
                      even
                      still
                      going on
                      going going going
                      soul
                      not killed
                      at death
                      still going
                      dead alive

still
not so clear
still around
still
ones you've known
not definite
you can't know
for sure
not one
can be sure
ever
sometimes clear

sometimes funny
sex
with someone else
you can never be sure
not only me
only me
myself
sometimes two
some one
sometimes two
sometimes only one
sometimes a woman
and a man
sometimes only one
either one
alone
jerking off
sometimes
sometimes not
sometimes God
sometimes only God
and sometimes
so many
someone else
only one time
self
sometimes two

sometimes music
delivers
it's beautiful
music
is great

so many things
so much can happen

open
open

music
can deliver

turning
deliver

something
something will clear
sometimes music
music
that will clear things
away
music
that will clear
the air

I died
the day I was born
and became an Angel
on that day

Since then
there are no days
there is no time
I am here
by mistake

Notes
    1. Martin Esslin, "Less Than the Sum of Its Parts," *American Theatre*
3:2(1986), 33.

-- 5 --

Reviews and Essays

Bernard Weiner, " 'Tongues':
A Poetic Exploration of Voices,"
San Francisco Chronicle, June 9, 1978

A black-shrouded chair (electric?). A man seated, talking. A poetic alien in a strange, arid land. Contemplation of death, the beauties of life, the waste of words. Behind him, unseen, sits another man, playing a multitude of percussive instruments.

It's "Tongues," the collaborative piece developed by Open Theatre founder-director Joseph Chaikin and playwright Sam Shepard—two giants in contemporary American drama—which had its world premiere Wednesday night at the Magic Theatre.

With only arms visible, Shepard accompanies Chaikin's mellifluous voice on bells, chimes, drums, maracas: a rhythm now fast, now slow, now aligned, now in syncopation, building a kind of jazz-theatre poem.

Chaikin as minimalist, a great admirer of Beckett's dark-comic explorations. Shepard as backup man, fascinated with music's ability to modify, suggest, expand mood of words.

"Tongues" reminds me of Shepard's "Killer's Head," a play that built an intense musical rhythm solely with words—also about a man in a chair, truly electric, having last thoughts just before being zapped into another dimension.

"Tongues" takes the man in the chair through various characters: lovers, eaters, job hunters, woman in labor, song singers, letter writers—some of it dark and somber, silence in hall, and some light and airy, with kids giggling at Chaikin's impersonations.

Part of his soliloquy reminds me of Emily Dickinson—with a fly, or in this case a mosquito, buzzing 'round her—as orchestrated by

Sun Ra. Other sections are reminiscent of Beckett world view or Pinter progressions: "a hunger so hungry that it's eating the hunger," "between this breath and the breath that's coming . . ." "when you die . . ."

"Tongues" ends with poetic affirmation, all the emptiness put in context. Chaikin intones that "today, people talked without speaking . . . tonight, I hear what the trees are saying."

There are two significant strains in contemporary American theatre; Shepard and Chaikin have roots in both, indeed are partially responsible for both.

One is usually called "new realism"—i.e., a shunning of post-war Absurdism in favor of a return to some forms of traditional naturalistic drama, at least as a takeoff point for more experimental explorations. One thinks of David Mamet, Albert Innaurato, Shepard's "Curse of the Starving Class," and so on.

The other is what might be termed "performance" theatre, ranging from the experiments of Robert Wilson ("Einstein on the Beach," "I Was Sitting on My Patio . . ."), Shepard ("Inacoma") and Chaikin ("Viet Rock") to "2019 Blake" by George Coates-Leonard Pitt and the one-man pieces by Winston Tong and others.

"Tongues" reflects both these strains and, as developed and expertly performed by Chaikin and Shepard, it is startlingly original and, though but thirty minutes long, is of great moment.

Bernard Weiner, "Squirming Permutations of Love," *San Francisco Chronicle*, September 8, 1979

"Savage/Love," the new Joseph Chaikin-Sam Shepard collaboration, which is having its world premiere at the Eureka Theatre here before heading off to New York, is a tantalizing, beautifully executed piece of musical theatre.

It is tantalizing in that it runs only thirty-five minutes, whetting one's appetite for more. It is musical theatre in the sense of verbal and instrumental jazz.

Shepard, its instigator and director, long has been fascinated with the many ways in which words can be emotionally embellished, illuminated, by musical accompaniment.

It's a preoccupation that goes back to such early plays as "Mad Dog Blues," through "The Tooth of Crime" and "Inacoma," up to last year's Chaikin-Shepard collaboration, "Tongues," which is playing in tandem with "Savage/Love" at the Eureka through tomorrow night.

It is difficult to imagine "Savage/Love" being as powerful as it is without the contributions of its accompanists, Harry Mann and Skip LaPlante, and without the carefully delineated performance of Chaikin.

In fact, careful crafting by Shepard and Chaikin exudes from every aspect of the play—including Beverly Emmons' expert lighting design—and, though the piece is short, it's crammed with vital theatre.

The title indicates its dual focus: the brutal and painful, the tender and romantic, aspects of love. It doesn't matter if one is male or female, gay or straight, shy or confident—"Savage/Love" speaks to any and all of those variables, a fact indicated by the nervous laughter in the opening night audience as Chaikin's monologues found their mark.

The form of the piece is that of a collage of brief scenes—in most of which characters portrayed by Chaikin speak directly to their lovers—punctuated and enhanced by Mann on sax or flute or clarinet, and LaPlante on a variety of "found" percussive instruments.

It opens with Chaikin wearing a nondescript postal worker's uniform—Mr. Everyman in love—describing, in terms of wonderment and rhapsody, how he met his mate-to-be.

A variety of characters follow: those afraid of being rejected, those pretending that the love relationship is stronger than it really is, those trying to invent new personalities and behavior patterns to please their lovers, those who mentally plot murder of their hated mates, those shy and pleading for attention, those haunted by a lost love, those who feel the numbness of estrangement, those preparing themselves for a love they have yet to meet, those who wake in the night just to drink in the vision of their love lying next to them, those jealous even of their mate's dream, those who find personal salvation in another being, those who want to communicate honestly to their mates but find it impossible.

All that and more, in short sketches that often generate laughs of recognition, but resound with something much more telling and serious.

There are two leitmotifs to the work. The characters constantly shift and move about—on, off, and around a bench-like protuberance in the corner of a room. The topic of love, and all its ramifications, makes them squirm, and no wonder: if you haven't squirmed, you haven't lived.

The other recurring pattern is the periodic appearance of a somewhat spastic character who tries desperately to convey his feelings to his lover, but gets all twisted up, physically and verbally, and simply can't get his message out in any but an excruciating manner.

But, as the piece closes, in a beautifully written and executed transition, the character suddenly blossoms into poetic speech, touched miraculously by love's magic: "I was shaking, you gave me your hand, from your fingers I returned: You, you, you . . ." A moving (almost Joycean) ending to a most entrancing work.

The contributions of Mann and, especially, LaPlante can't be overstated. The former, on recognizable horns, provides rhythms, accompaniments. Just prior to a nervous monologue, for example, Mann delivers a crescendo on the flute; later, he uncorks a saxophone "rush" to accompany a murder wish.

LaPlante provides more ethereal moods, resonances. Chaikin speaks of a scene at the water, for example, and LaPlante creates a tabla-like bubble sound, using a peanut butter jar half filled with liquid. At other moments, he bows concave pieces of mirror, or creates gong effects by striking oven grills, or passes his hand along wind chimes made of nails. The effect is strikingly original and emotionally evocative.

LaPlante is also the percussionist in "Tongues"—a role filled by Shepard last year—and will be performing in both pieces in New York.

Chaikin is a marvel to watch, in both pieces. With a simple relaxation or tensing of his voice, or part of his face or body or eyes, he creates a multiplicity of characters and emotions.

There is one three-part scene where he goes from a self-demeaning beggar for love to a denouncer of his love object—and, in each of the segments, he is totally believable, with no hint of what is to come, and yet the transitions are palpably there, somehow. It's virtuoso magic.

In another scene, a character, perhaps strait-jacketed in an asylum, whispers the pain of loss to his love, that "you are missing from the places you lived in me."

Love can do that to you, exult you, fill you with delicious joy, and it can drag you down as well, into the pits of despondency, even madness. The accomplishment of "Savage/Love" is the way it manages to capture both aspects of that state in a seemingly simple but intricately worked-out form.

Thanks to the Magic Theatre and Eureka Theatre Company for producing these collaborations by two of America's foremost theatre artists.

James Leverett, "Other Voices," *The Soho Weekly News*, November 22, 1979

You probably don't have to be told to go see a collaboration between Sam Shepard and Joseph Chaikin. The names are enough. One is the best American playwright of his generation, the other, through his work as a director and actor, has changed the way we make theatre. But "Tongues" and "Savage/Love," their two performance-music pieces now at the Public Theatre, are not just excuses for two names to appear on the same program. The joys, surprises, and weaknesses of the works lie in the fact that these talents have truly combined with one another.

If there is a dominant partner in this marriage, it is surely Chaikin. Elsewhere Shepard has given us richer, more exciting, challenging material. But nowhere has Chaikin shown greater mastery of an acting technique so original, personal, and compelling that it can be referred to as an aesthetic, almost a philosophy. It is as though Shepard had recognized a special moment in his partner's creativity and stepped back; or better, allowed himself to become transparent in order to let it come through. What emerges is the pure presence of an extraordinary actor—mature, classic in its economy, consummate in its power.

This presence expresses itself musically and lyrically, which is also the way Shepard works when he is closest to his talent. *Tongues* is the apt title for the whole program as well as for one of the pieces. Each work is an orchestration of voices riding through on the breath of a single actor. "Savage/Love" is a composition (but not a story) about the many facets of love. "Tongues" has a broader scope—birth, appetite, love, death—but it is assembled in essentially the same way.

Both owe a debt to Samuel Beckett, particularly to pieces like

"Come and Go" and "Play," in which a polyphony of fragmented personae utter feelings, dreams, memories until a tapestry has been woven. In it one can follow not only purely thematic motifs but also the elliptical yet tenacious traces of specific life stories. If anything, Shepard/Chaikin's works are even more abstract and free of the idea of narrative (though, paradoxically, also more directly emotional and accessible). Beckett may be their literary ancestor, but their more immediate inspiration is jazz. Chaikin is as much an instrument in a combo as an actor in a play. The rhythms, timbres, and gestures of the characters that come through him have a musical as well as dramatic value and function. He becomes the lead player to a backup of horns and percussion in the first piece, and to a still wider variety of percussion in the second. And still closer to these pieces than either Beckett or jazz is Chaikin's own work with the Open Theatre (with which Shepard was associated). The transformational style developed by this seminal group allows the actor, and behind him the playwright, to become a poet—the one voice through which many may speak— or, to use an image near and dear to Shepard, a shaman through whom many spirits may manifest themselves.

Some Shepard fans will probably object to "Savage/Love" because the writer has put himself so thoroughly at the service of the performer. The text contains none of the mythic resonances and poetic flights that mark vintage Shepard. The words are surprisingly simple and direct—like the lyrics of a popular song. Like a song, they are occasionally a bit precious and overly sentimental. Their sole purpose is to provide a score or repertoire for Chaikin, and like a popular singer, he becomes *the* lover by containing many lovers. He has the quality of a great interpreter: he is an innocent, vulnerable, receptive, blank where new love, used love, dead love all have their say.

"Tongues" is much more Shepard's piece. Perhaps this is in part because he was the percussionist in the original production in San Francisco, sitting directly behind Chaikin so that only his bare arms could be seen as he reached for one instrument, struck, or shook another. The placement itself is quintessentially Shepard in what it evokes poetically: a many-armed seer, a two-faced god. The language is characteristic too, but with unmistakable overtones of the Open Theatre: a riff on eating, the incantations of a medicine man, speculations on death, the amazement of a new mother. Yet

Chaikin unmistakably occupies the center. The words are no less his for sounding more like Shepard. It is still he, the actor, losing his voice among many voices.

As for the music other than the words, much of it is by Shepard, an untutored but natural musician. There is also additional material and live accompaniment by Skip LaPlante (percussion) and Harry Mann (horns). Perhaps it is Shepard's own innocent directness about music that makes the score for "Savage/Love" often funny and funky. Surely LaPlante's own experience with his collective, "Music for Homemade Pieces," enriched the percussive variety of both pieces.

Another important musical element is Beverly Emmons' lighting, particularly in "Savage/Love," where it picks up every change of mood—that is, change of voice—swiftly, subtly, and with variety. Finally, Robert Woodruff, who has directed so many important Shepard productions, brings great strength and definition to these small pieces without ever letting on that they are directed at all.

Mel Gussow, From "Intimate Monologues That Speak to the Mind and Heart," *The New York Times*, December 9, 1979

. . . For years, Mr. Chaikin and Mr. Shepard have been friends and mutual admirers, and recently they joined creative forces. The result, *Tongues*, currently running at the Public Theatre, is not only an exquisite piece of performance theatre, it is, to a great extent, a consolidation, a précis of the work of these two extraordinary theatre artists over a span of fifteen years.

The evening is composed of two monologues, "Savage/Love" and the title piece. They are completely a collaborative effort between Mr. Chaikin and Mr. Shepard. Although it is probably pointless to divide authorship, for the record, "Savage/Love" was written by Mr. Shepard and "Tongues" by Mr. Shepard and Mr. Chaikin. Music for both plays was composed by Mr. Shepard, Skip LaPlante, and Harry Mann, and is played by the last two at the Public. The only actor on stage is Mr. Chaikin, and the evening is directed by Robert Woodruff. Many hands, one voice.

These are interior monologues, daydreams, and nightmares, communicated as from analysand to analyst. The actor exposes

his emotions and recapitulates his life. We become his confidant—
and we are enthralled. The last line of "Tongues," "Tonight I am
learning its language"—the language being that of death—is the
key to both halves of this abstract evening. In "Savage/Love," we
listen to, and learn, the language of love. The overall title refers
to language as well as speech. Each play is a poem, or rather a
series of poems, centering on a single subject. They are one-man
versions of what the Open Theatre ensemble did in "Terminal"
and "Nightwalk," two pieces that are the antecedents of the current
evening.

The environment at the Public is a niche in a brick wall, set for
sleep. In "Savage/Love," Mr. Chaikin twists and turns, fighting for
sleep. He is restless to the extreme, and we can feel that his mind
and his memory are as tangled as his limbs and his bedclothes.
Gradually his soliloquy takes form. He leads us through a love
story from first meeting to courtship, romance and sexual fulfillment, and then shows us first doubt, competitiveness, rising jealousy
and symbolic murder. The love story becomes more savage and
also more of a performance. The lovers are aware of the roles
that they are playing, of the compromises that they are making in
search of compatability. "Now one of us is acting the pain of
premonition," says Mr. Chaikin. He carries us through to parting,
regret, remorse, and renewal. Interspersed are the sounds of sleep.
Occasionally the actor babbles as if talking in his sleep. Wistfully
he sings, "I'm in the mood for love," and with balletic grace, he
physicalizes his longing and his distress. The soliloquy is beautifully
counterpointed by a jazz score, played by Mr. LaPlante and Mr.
Mann—a tapestry of mellifluous words and music.

In the second and title piece, Mr. Chaikin is sitting, as if propped
up in bed, or installed on a throne. Behind him in back of a screen
is Mr. LaPlante playing an orchestra of finger instruments. His
bare arms jut out, clanging cymbals and cowbells, striking bongos
and maracas, and rubbing the rims of bowls so that they make
musical sounds. The authors subtitle their play, "a piece for voice
and percussion," and it is an articulate collaboration between actor
and musician. Mr. Chaikin resembles an Indian god, or perhaps,
because of his youthful face, a child as god, and the musician's
arms appear to extend as appendages from the actor's body.

"Tongues" is a collage of echoes from the dead. It is as if the
speaker is conducting his own death ritual, as if he is an attendant
at his wake. Feverishly he tries to remember life, and darts all the

way back to birth. He "leaves" his body and circumnavigates his soul. We hear the voices of hunger and voices of those who have died. The piece is mystical and it is also intensely personal; much of it was apparently inspired by Mr. Chaikin's own open-heart surgery. In one section, with a certain amount of humor, he signs off, naming various kinds of endings from "all my love" to "forever." Despite the subject matter, "Tongues" is not depressing. It pulsates with the heartbeat of life.

Although the two works can be read as poetry, they are chiefly plays to be performed, and, once seen, they are inseparable from the performance. Mr. Chaikin is the ideal interpreter. His voice, face, and body become conductors of expression. In *Tongues*, he offers one of those rare one-man performances in which a stage seems richly and densely populated.

NOTE: The following letter, dated December 7, 1979, corrects a few errors in the above article.

Dear Mel Gussow:

My warmest thanks for your pieces on *Tongues*. I had no clear idea at all how anyone would respond to the pieces, and I appreciated your insight and enthusiasm.

There were two points you made which make me feel that you must have been given the wrong impression by someone. One was that you said "for the record" that Sam and I wrote "Tongues" and that Sam wrote "Savage/Love." That wasn't the working process. In behalf of Sam, I can securely say that we collaborated equally on "Savage/Love"; in fact, if it were measurable, I had a little less to do with the writing of "Tongues" and more on "Savage/Love."

The other point is that "Tongues" was inspired by my heart surgery. My major heart surgery occurred after I worked on "Tongues," although illness and medical problems have followed me intermittently since I was a child. I was unknowingly very ill while I was working on "Tongues." The theme of death and dying has come up for me in many different works; only in *Terminal* was it meant to be central. Its meaning and interest in the theatre for me is less as autobiography than as a common fate. Because theatre is about live people in a room, it is a meeting point.

With best wishes,

Joseph Chaikin

Bernard Weiner, "Curtain Calls,"
San Francisco Chronicle, February 19, 1986

Joseph Chaikin, one of the leading theatre artists in America, suffered a stroke in 1984. He lost use of the right side of his body and virtually all of his speech.

Since that time, he's regained use of his right side and has come a long way in terms of his speech. He has trouble talking in conversation, but he's fairly adept at reading from a text.

Sunday night, for one performance only, Chaikin read and performed a piece he co-wrote with his friend and colleague Sam Shepard, "The War in Heaven," that spoke directly to Chaikin's journey back from death and disability.

Virtually everybody who is anybody in Bay Area drama was on hand, both to pay homage to Chaikin, one of the great theatrical innovators and teachers, and to hear yet another of the Chaikin-Shepard collaborations. (They had premiered "Tongues" and "Savage/Love" in San Francisco.)

The twenty-five-minute reading was an exceptionally moving one. Here was Chaikin, with his mellifluous voice rising and falling, having difficulty pronouncing certain words, while telling us what was, symbolically, the story of his return from the dead.

"I'm here by mistake," he tells us early on. "I'm not sure where I fit." He was on a mission, then suddenly, "in a moment of doubt, I crashed to earth." He wound up, as an angel, in heaven.

Every second he remains there, he feels as if he is weakening. "Turn me loose," he shouts, leaning toward the audience. "Take me back."

He talks about the glories and mysteries of air, sex, love, God, constantly punctuating his litany with the plaintive refrain: "Turn me loose."

"I've been dead and born so many times," he says, and now it's time once again for a new beginning. He has a partner in this new adventure. "The partner is me."

The audience erupted into applause. Joe's back with us, if not yet at the height of his powers, at least on the road to recovery, still willing and eager to explore the world's wonders in theatrical terms.

Robert Everett-Green, "Chaikin Speaks in the
Voice of an Angel," *The Globe and Mail* (Toronto),
June 13, 1986

. . . "The War in Heaven" is the poetic testimony of an angel who
has somehow, "in a moment of doubt," tumbled to earth. What
he would like very much is to get back, as he explains during a
brilliantly evocative twenty-minute monologue that ranges freely
over heaven and earth. Chaikin's angel is a prisoner, "weakening
every second I'm here," but he is no heroic junior god, no
Prometheus bound to a rock. He is one of heaven's foot soldiers,
a childlike functionary who looks on man and God from almost
equal distance.

"The War in Heaven" was originally written for radio, so there
was nothing amiss in seeing Chaikin play it sitting in a chair in the
middle of an empty stage, reading his part from a music stand.
"Reading" is an entirely inadequate word to describe this performance, even disregarding the intense effort required for Chaikin
to hold the resistant words together. Often the words sprang up
glittering and alive like the fragments of light which, in the Hasidic
scheme of things, are all that remain of a primordial unity, and
whose reunion is the main work of every believer. Chaikin's
rhythmic phrasing and his mobile facial gestures fused into a
compelling whole the frequently scattered musings of the angel,
who breaks off time and again to plead for freedom and return.

One uncharacteristically long anecdote described "a battalion"
of angels coming down to fetch the soul of a great man. They
waited by the bier and then at the cemetery and consulted nervously
with each other before concluding that the man had none. Back
in heaven, they made their report—"and they told us we must
have been mistaken." End of story—a tremendously funny story
when followed up by Chaikin's look of naive amazement.

Director Steven Kent has provided the stage version of "The
War in Heaven" with a quick-changing play of light to complement
the spare percussion score devised by Shepard. Kent also acted as
interpreter for a brief interview with Chaikin after the performance.

In conversation, the aphasia dogs him heavily, dragging down
his thought, and the words bubble up slowly from his chest.

"Thinking . . . too much now . . . too big emotionally now," Chaikin says. He defers to Kent, who says that, as the words have receded, Chaikin's emotional sensitivity has grown tremendously. Always passionately interested in engaging his audience, he now grasps even more urgently for the messages of eyes, the eyes in the theatre. "This theatre . . . better for that," he says.

William Kleb, "Shepard and Chaikin: Speaking in Tongues," *Theatre* 10:1

In a recent statement in *Theater* (Spring, 1978), Sam Shepard argued for a more flexible attitude towards theatrical "time": form—"the total experience of the piece (including its length)"—cannot be separated from content; the work itself, its peculiar energy, declares the track it must follow; the shorter work, therefore, is not necessarily inferior to the "full-length." *Tongues*, presented by San Francisco's Magic Theatre for five nights only (June 7–11, 1978), offered a vivid demonstration of this thesis.

Developed collaboratively by Shepard and Joseph Chaikin (who was brought to San Francisco as part of the Rockefeller grant which supported this project), and performed entirely by them, the "theater piece" lasted a little over half an hour. Nothing else was offered to fill out the evening. The minimal visual format of the work matched its length. Throughout, Chaikin performed seated on a throne-like chair at the center of the small proscenium stage, facing front; Shepard sat directly behind him, cross-legged on a low platform, facing upstage. Chaikin, wearing a simple blue shirt and dark slacks, remained motionless for the most part; a colorful Mexican blanket covered his legs, as if he were an invalid, unable to walk; his hands rested quietly in his lap; he moved his head occasionally as he spoke and his expression changed as he assumed different characters or attitudes. Behind Chaikin, various percussive musical instruments were arranged on the low platform (a snare drum, a cymbal, bongos, gourd rattles, sticks, bells), and Shepard played these, rhythmically accompanying Chaikin's words. Only Shepard's bare, sinewy arms were visible as he reached out to pick up and play the different instruments; his movements seemed stylized, choreographed, and the effect was as though Chaikin were four-armed Vishnu telling his dreams.

These "dreams"—a sequence of about a dozen monologues, soliloquies, and one dialogue (both parts played by Chaikin), none lasting more than two or three minutes—made up the text of "Tongues." Actually, it was not clear who or what the Chaikin/ Shepard figure was—dreamer, icon, storyteller, invalid, actor, dying man, or all of these—but the overall impression was one of voices in space, disembodied tongues, words and music, speaking through this unitary, oracular presence. Many of the words spoken were serious, solemn, and a number of the sections dealt with death and the moment of dying. For instance, the piece opened with a fragmented third-person narrative (reminiscent of Beckett's *Not I*) in which "a voice" comes to a man in a dream saying, "You are entirely dead. What is unfinished is forever unfinished. What has happened has happened. You are entirely gone from the people." Then, about halfway through the piece, another passage occurred, accompanied ritualistically by tinkling bells, which also seemed to describe the moment of dying: "There was this moment where I vanished . . . There was this moment that passed, taking me with it." And again, near the end, a character (doctor, friend, relative?) decided to "make something up" in an apparent attempt to comfort someone about to die—a rapid litany of all the final guesses, each beginning with the phrase, "When you die . . ."

This recurrent preoccupation with dying at first seemed to suggest that the other "voices" in "Tongues," those not dealing with this subject, were meant to be the random thoughts or memories of a man (the sleeper in the first section) at the moment of death. But, unlike Shepard's *Killer's Head* (a monologue delivered by a man strapped to an electric chair), these utterances, many of them comic or ironic, came from a variety of characters (hyped-up job hunter, dim-witted letter writer, cliché-bound politician) and, finally, they did not seem clearly enough related to the consciousness of the dying man to make such a literal interpretation consistent or convincing. At one point, for instance, a woman spoke of her amazement at the pain of childbirth and of her wonder at the newborn creature in her arms; at another, a dialogue between two people trying to decide if they're hungry began as an amusing parody of Pinter (perhaps even of Shepard himself in *Action*), then shifted abruptly into an obsessive, rhythmic chant about an all-consuming hunger that would, eventually, devour itself.

Nevertheless, "Tongues" did not seem fragmented in performance. The Chaikin/Shepard figure, ambiguous though it was, provided a powerful visual matrix, while Chaikin's remarkable voice, though it changed, sometimes radically, from section to section, bound the individual speeches together musically and as the sole source of the words. In fact, before "Tongues" opened, Shepard announced that it would be "based on conversations to do with the role of the voice" and this, finally, seemed to be the unifying theme.

On the most obvious level, the text itself presented a variety of dramatic voices and, from the actor's point of view, vocal possibilities: all three tenses were used; while most characters were men, at least one was obviously a woman; age and attitude seemed to vary widely. Also, many if not all the sections referred specifically in some way or another to a voice or voices. However, human voices often seemed to deal with the inadequacies of speech, its inability to express true meaning:

> They told me what kind of pain I'd have
> . . .
> [But] nothing they told me was like this.
>
> It's like I'm never gonna find my voice
> again.
> Ever again.
>
> It's not often, actually, that I find myself at
> a loss for words
>
> I don't know what to tell you exactly,
> I don't wanna lie to you.
>
> Hi! There. That's me. Me. Saying, Hi! To
>   myself . . .
> Why should I doubt it? Not me? Who else
>   could it have been?

On the other hand, non-human voices, from other planes, and from nature, seemed associated with more profound or intense forms of communication, beyond the power of words, on a level of intuition and pure feeling:

> In this dream, a voice speaks.
>
> Between the breath I'm breathing
> And the one that's coming.
> Something tells me now.

Today, the wind roared through the
center
    of town.
Tonight, I hear its voice . . .
Today, the tree bloomed without a word.
Tonight, I'm learning its language.

Not surprisingly, these voices turned out to be the most eloquent
in "Tongues"; paradoxically perhaps, they offered vivid proof of
the power of words both to evoke concrete pictures in the mind
and to create rich tonal harmonies and complex rhythmic patterns.
Indeed, the use of sound in these passages seemed especially
important: in many of the sections dealing with specific characters,
the sound of the language was emphasized principally as a way to
define character: in these more mystical sections, however, it was
clearly intended to function as a kind of chant, a mantric spell
which might focus and release energies contained within the words
themselves, and which might even, given the right vibrations,
summon the actual "tongues."

   This, Shepard has said, is precisely the aspect of language that
interests him the most as a playwright ("words as living incantations
not as symbols") and he has described his own process in just such
mediumistic terms:

> In my experience the character is visualized, he appears out of
> nowhere in three dimensions and speaks. He doesn't speak to me
> because I'm not in the play. I'm watching it. He speaks to something
> or someone else, or even to himself, or even to no one. . . . In other
> words, I'm taking notes in as much detail as possible on an event
> that's happening somewhere inside me. (*The Drama Review*, Decem-
> ber 1977)

As Chaikin sees it, the role of the actor's "voice" is similar;
through a "balancing between very specific technical disciplines
and mysterious areas having to do with breathing rhythm and
space," he attempts to speak a language which is "three-dimen-
sional," not simply a "flat label"; to do this with true emotional
resonance he must turn inward and "liberate" those sounds closed
up inside:

> Ultimately, acting is to be able to speak in the tongues of the
> tortured, assassinated, betrayed, starving parts of ourselves impris-
> oned in the disguise of the "setup." And to locate and liberate those
> voices which sing from the precious buried parts of ourselves where

we are bewildered and alive beyond business matters, in irreducible radiance. (*The Presence of the Actor*, 1972)

Thus, on another level, "Tongues" seemed an obvious declaration of aesthetic principles. The fact that Chaikin and Shepard performed the piece themselves, of course, merely emphasized this, while the closeness of their respective attitudes (the ideal collaborative relationship between actor and playwright) was vividly dramatized by the fused iconic presence they created together on stage. Chaikin as actor, visible and vocal, front and center; Shepard as writer, practically invisible behind him, but literally backing him up. The two, in effect, functioning as one. In short, not only did the staging of "Tongues" visibly embody a shared vision of the role of the artist (actor and playwright), the rigorously pared-down form perfectly expressed the overall content of the work. And this seemed by no means slight or inconsequential.

Ironically, it seems unlikely that "Tongues" will ever be staged again, but it has been recorded as part of the Radio Arts Project and will be broadcast in the Bay Area, and, RAP hopes, elsewhere, sometime in 1979.

Doris Auerbach, "Speaking in Tongues: Exploring the Inner Library," From *Sam Shepard, Arthur Kopit and the Off Broadway Theatre*.

In the summer of 1978, Shepard returned to the collaborative process with which he had first worked in the late 1960s and with which he had experimented in 1977 in *Inacoma*. Shepard had known and respected Joseph Chaikin for over fifteen years and had approached him with the idea that they "build a piece together."[1] Chaikin came to San Francisco, and in three weeks they had created "Tongues," a one-act play which, together with "Savage/Love," opened to enthusiastic reviews in November 1979 at the Public Theatre in New York. The two one-act plays explore the language of love and death.

Shepard drew together in these two short plays two themes that had concerned him during his fifteen years of playwriting—the relationship of music to words in the theatre, and the inadequacy of language to express emotion. The collective title of the two plays is *Tongues*, which refers to both language and speech. While this seems to put Shepard—who chose the title—right in the midst of structural linguistics and its distinction between *la langue*, the abstract system of language, and *la parole*, the concrete, individual utterances we refer to as speech,[2] the playwright denies this. "Ideas like 'structuralism' are completely foreign to me."[3] Yet Shepard has long been fascinated by the very personal reference each writer has to language; a concern he has explored in "The Inner Library" article, which tries to express the inner territory which language attempts to chart. Despite Shepard's denials, his concern with the very personal associations that exist between words that a writer chooses brings his thinking close to that of de Saussure, who wrote of "the inner storehouse that makes up the language of each speaker."[4]

Shepard writes eloquently of what motivated him and Chaikin in the creation of the play:

> If we talk seriously about the content of *Tongues* there's no point in trying to fix it into a concept of theatre. Our approach was always from the angle of experience. By that I mean "what is it like" to be in the multiplicity of situations that love calls us to. "What is it like" to be the beggar of love, the killer of love, etc. From there by deeply submerging oneself into the predicament come all the questions, all the language, all the form. Not from the head. The head, at best, can only make up theories, and theories don't hold water if experience defies them. This is the territory we were working in. I'm not at all interested in conceptual art. It's barren and void of true meaning. People are not moved toward their life by theories and concepts. If theatre is to have any meaning it must touch people where they live, not where they think they think. True thought only comes from opening to areas of experience that ordinary thought is too dull to grasp. So this opens lots of questions that appear very simplistic but have to be answered to. Mainly, what is experience and what is thought? To be more specific in regard to *Tongues*, the questions were, what is the experiene of love in domains that we felt hadn't been addressed? Moments of almost paralyzing doubt and wonder. What is the thought that can reach into that world and depict its mystery?[5]

What Shepard and Chaikin were trying to delve into is what Goethe called "incommensurable," the relation between chaotic feeling and shaped artistic form.

"*Tongues*"

The first of the two one-act plays is "Tongues." Its theme is death and dying. This focus came about partly from the creators' "interest in expressing extreme conditions, partly from an idea they had early on to structure the pieces as a fantasy of the past lives of a dying man—and partly from the fact that Chaikin literally was in heart failure."[6] In fact, when Chaikin returned to New York, he underwent open-heart surgery. He has recovered from this ordeal and put in a stellar performance as the solo actor in the Public Theatre's production of the two monologues with music which make up *Tongues*. Chaikin recalls, "I was very weak when we were working on 'Tongues.' Extremely sick, and I didn't know it."[7]

Since they presented the one-acter "Tongues" in the summer of 1978 at the Magic Theatre in San Francisco, Chaikin's weak physical condition determined the staging, which calls for the actor to sit almost motionless on stage: "an image suggesting illness and also somehow, a priest or medium through whom voices come."[8] The austere, static, onstage performance belies the peripatetic creation of the play, which was composed all over the city of San Francisco. "Sam likes egg foo yung, so we'd go to this Chinese restaurant, or we'd go to the park or to the zoo,"[9] Chaikin recollects. Since they worked all about the town, Chaikin remembers that deciding where they would eat became a daily ritual. Perhaps their daily conversations about food led Shepard once again brilliantly to use hunger as a metaphor. Shepard writes that they generalized "from that particular mundane hunger for food to many aspects of hunger, hunger of different levels. Fat people want more than just steaks."[10]

In "Tongues," a piece described as being for voice and percussion, the character in a long "aria" speaks of a hunger that consumes him. "Nothing I ate could satisfy this hunger I'm having right now."[11]

This metaphor of spiritual hunger can be traced right through Shepard's plays. It becomes most agonizing in this long monologue delivered alone on a stage by a man barely moving a muscle. With the exception of the very short *Killer Head* (presented together with *Action* at the American Place Theatre), Shepard until now has explored humanity's problem of existential loneliness against a background of society where an attempt, even though unsuccessful, to communicate can be made. In "Tongues," the aloneness of death is brilliantly brought to the audience's attention, as the actor feverishly tries to recall his life going back to birth; but the play becomes a death ritual.

"Savage/Love"

While the solitude in "Tongues" helps him learn the language of death, helps him administer his own death rites, the actor is equally alone in "Savage/Love." It is an interesting commentary on Shepard's perception of love. Surely the language of love is difficult, if not impossible, to learn alone, in isolation. Despite his quest for attachment and commitment, the lover in "Savage/Love" sees love as more of a power struggle than anything else. The powerful image of killing that Shepard uses focuses on the hatred inherent in love, on the doubt, competitiveness, and jealousy leading to its symbolic murder.

Music is an integral part of *Tongues*. The playbill for the Public Theatre's production states, "In one way, both of these collaborations are an attempt to find an equal expression between music and the actor. They are like environments where the words and gestures are given temporary atmospheres to breathe in through sound and rhythm." The plays are in fact structurally much closer to musical compositions than to plays. "Rather than having beginnings, middles, and ends, plots and consistent characters, they are built with themes that are stated, developed, and counterpointed."[12]

Sam Shepard has left behind, for the time being, his overwhelming involvement with the land and the dream, which he summed up in *Buried Child*, and has turned to the universals of death and love. The stark aloneness of the lover on a mattress crying out to a nonexistent partner: "Will you give me some part of yourself?" underlines Shepard's continuing concern for the individual's isolation on this cold star of an earth. Perhaps only a renewal of faith in the viability of the American dream can assuage the despair.

Notes

1. Eileen Blumenthal, "Chaikin and Shepard Speak in Tongues," *Village Voice*, November 26, 1979, p. 103.
2. Terence Hawkes, *Structuralism and Semiotics* (Berkeley and Los Angeles, 1977), p. 20.
3. From an unpublished letter to the author dated 12/7/79.
4. Hawkes, p. 27.
5. From an unpublished letter to the author dated 1/11/80.
6. Blumenthal, p. 108.
7. Ibid.
8. Ibid.
9. Ibid.
10. Ibid., p. 103.
11. Ibid.
12. Ibid., p. 109.

Eileen Blumenthal, "Sam Shepard and Joseph Chaikin: Speaking in Tongues," From *American Dreams: The Imagination of Sam Shepard*, Bonnie Marranca, ed.

Joseph Chaikin sits on a high-backed chair, gazing toward the audience. His hands rest on the Mexican blanket covering his lap. Unseen maracas begin a tempo, and Chaikin starts to speak. Occasionally, a bare arm holding the maracas reaches out from behind the chair to accent a beat—the split-second image vaguely suggesting a multi-limbed Hindu god. For the next half hour, Chaikin remains nearly motionless, while a dozen voices come through him: the tongues of people dying, giving birth, wrestling with passion and wonder, or just trying to make it through the day.

"Tongues" is the first of two monologues with music which Chaikin and Sam Shepard created. The second is a biting, affecting, funny piece called "Savage/Love." Both works came from intensive explorations of language, sound, and the power of an actor to transmit extreme conditions. More basically, they are the fruit of a long-term desire by two of the most innovative artists in American theatre to collaborate with each other.

Shepard and Chaikin met at a dinner party in 1964. Shepard,

at that point, had written mostly poetry and was just starting to focus on plays; Chaikin had already received recognition as an actor, had directed a little, and was the dominant figure in the fledging Open Theater. "We really had a rapport," Chaikin recalls. "After the dinner, we walked a long distance together along some highway, and we talked. And I told him to come to a workshop at the Open Theater." (Except as noted, all quotations come from my interviews and conversations with Chaikin and Shepard—Chaikin in person, Shepard via long-distance telephone—in November 1979.) Shepard was around the edges of the company, then, for the rest of its existence: "I went to a lot of workshops. Every once in a while, Joe asked me to write something and I would do it. I was always like in and out, contributing to the work just in little particles, in little pieces." In 1966, he wrote *Icarus's Mother*, which was performed by Open Theater actors. Later, he created three monologues for *Terminal*, "Cowboy," "Stone Man," and "Teleported Man." (None was finally used; they are published in Shepard's *Hawk Moon*.) And he wrote several key speeches and scenes for *Nightwalk*. But while Chaikin thinks of Shepard as one of the writers who nourished the Open Theater, Shepard (like all of the company's writers except, perhaps, Jean-Claude van Itallie) always felt uneasy, on the periphery: "I never knew my place in the Open Theater, you know? I didn't have a place in the Open Theater. I was hanging out with different people, and I would come by. I felt a kinship with Joe. But I didn't know how to function as a writer there at all."

After the Open Theater disbanded, Shepard suggested to Chaikin that they create a piece together, and in the summer of 1978, Chaikin went to San Francisco to work with Shepard for a month. They had decided to proceed without an ensemble—to make something between the two of them which Chaikin would then perform. Although they had exchanged letters about the area they wanted to explore, and Shepard already had suggested the title "Tongues," they had no specific themes and no usable text when Chaikin arrived—"almost nothing," Shepard says, "but a desire to work together."

After three weeks of intensive conversations, writing, and rehearsals, "Tongues," a piece for voice (Chaikin's) and percussion (played by Shepard), was ready for an audience. The following summer, after a dozen more letters back and forth, they worked for three weeks developing "Savage/Love"—this time using an actor's (Chaikin's) voice, percussion, and horns.

The collaboration periods were so brief, Chaikin explains, because "Sam has an aversion to New York, and he's terrified of flying, and I couldn't stay for too long." (*New York Times*, January 13, 1980) The work could move quickly, though, "because there was so much water under the bridge between Sam and me," because of the years they'd known each other both as artists and friends. The lack of an ensemble also made the process very efficient. Only two people, rather than Chaikin's usual eight to twenty, were exploring each idea. And since there weren't actors' egos to be protected, sections that seemed barren could be abandoned quickly and ruthlessly.

Despite some specific disagreements, Chaikin and Shepard never found themselves at odds over the basic nature of the work. At first this seems strange, because their theatre apart from these collaborations had been very different from one another's. Shepard's plays had mostly been flashy, kaleidoscopic trips—chemical, musical, psychological, or literal—through very personal, mid- and western-American terrain. Chaikin's had been intense, distilled collages about mythic-scope themes such as dying and human mutability. Still, Chaikin and Shepard had often been on parallel tracks. Each had tried to express inner territory. And each had explored the relationships between language and music—how words can produce different voices and modes, how musical elements, including structure, can be adapted to the theatre.

A big factor in making the collaboration click was Chaikin and Shepard's mutual respect and affection. Neither their egos nor their sensibilities clashed. Chaikin says he kept expecting to find boundaries beyond which they couldn't relate to each other's experiences, but those obstacles just didn't materialize. There was only one tiny area where an impulse of Shepard's was foreign to him. ("Savage/Love" has a line about wanting to die before one's lover; for Chaikin, who has suffered a critical heart condition since childhood, this was unfamiliar.) Chaikin *wanted* to include that line in the piece, though, to try to enter its realm of emotion. And, he says, "Although it's possible that Sam also had feelings about certain things being very strange, I don't think so. My impression was that he didn't." Asked if he had felt pressed into someone else's way of seeing—particularly since these joint creations are closer in form and mood to Chaikin's work than to his—Shepard said that his enormous respect for Chaikin prevented that from being an issue:

> When you're collaborating with someone who you can learn from, it's very different from collaborating with someone who you're struggling with in some kind of competitive way. Like you're showing each other your chops. Musicians call it chops. If you can play a scale sixteen ways, you've got chops—and there are ways of playing together where you show that off. But when you're working with someone who actually has an experience that penetrates deeply, and you know you can learn from it, the relationship isn't that way. I feel like I'm an apprentice to Joe. I don't feel that in any kind of pejorative way, like a servant, but—I feel like he's my elder. So there's no problem with me in terms of feeling like his ideas are infringing on my vision.

Another thing that facilitated the collaboration was that Shepard and Chaikin were accomplished in several areas of theatre. Chaikin was an experienced actor and director as well as a leader of experimental workshops and ensemble creations. Shepard, in addition to writing, had directed, performed in, and composed music for his plays, and had recently acted in a Hollywood film. And although he had mostly written alone, he had contributed to the Open Theater and had collaborated with Patti Smith on *Cowboy Mouth*, so joint playwriting was not new to him.

The functions of playwright, director, and composer melded in the San Francisco work. Shepard says: "The actual material of the thing doesn't break down so easily into who did the words and who did the music; for me, it really was a collaboration in the truest sense. Nobody can really lay claim to any one aspect. The words were both of ours really." Chaikin agrees, though he adds that because Shepard "is a writer the rest of the time, in that sense I feel like he was the custodian of the words." Chaikin credits Shepard with having directed "Savage/Love" and, for the most part, "Tongues." (Robert Woodruff came in to help direct "Tongues" in San Francisco when Shepard began performing the music and directed both plays for the subsequent productions.) But Shepard says, "In a way, Joe directed from the inside."

Chaikin and Shepard began work on "Tongues" by trying to explore a kind of expression Chaikin could not quite define but called "thought music." In the early stages, they used a simple story as a provisional springboard and structure. Chaikin recalls:

The first idea, which was thrown away but is in the piece anyway, was "Let's make up this thing about a person who died and had many other lives. And make a fantasy of the lives." So that's where we started from. Although we departed entirely from that idea, it gave a really very nice trampoline for us to play with.

For several weeks they worked in different places around San Francisco: "Sam likes egg foo yung, so we'd go to this Chinese restaurant, or we'd go to the park or to the zoo, or we'd stay in my hotel room." Through conversations, they would focus on an area, a kind of voice that they wanted to include in the work. Then, Chaikin explains:

We would sit there and make something up. I'd sometimes make up a line, he'd follow it; he'd make up a line, I'd follow it. Or sometimes he would write something and read it back to me, and I would say why I didn't want to go in that direction or why I didn't think it was such an interesting direction or—you know how I like everything to be distilled, how I can't stand anything that spreads— I'd say why it would be better like that.

The resulting texts often mixed Chaikin's and Shepard's impulses. One section, for example, sprang from Chaikin's account of being with a friend who had come out of brain surgery almost totally blind. But Chaikin's manner of description was fused with an image that really was from Shepard's America: "In front of you is a window. About chest level. It's night out . . . On the wall are pictures from your past. One is a photograph. You as a boy. You standing in front of a cactus. You're wearing a red plaid shirt . . . A mosquito races around your ear. The same mosquito you're hearing."

Some voices in the piece came directly from Chaikin and Shepard's experiences during the collaboration. For example, since they worked all over the city, deciding when and where to eat became a daily ritual of almost comic mutual politeness. One day, their talk about eating led to a long discussion about hunger. They generalized, Shepard recalls, "from that particular mundane hunger for food to many aspects of hunger, hunger on different levels. Fat people, for example, want more than just steaks." After that conversation, Chaikin told me, "Sam went home and wrote, and came in the next day with this speech which was, more or less, the way it is in the final piece."

It begins with a dialogue (both voices performed by Chaikin):—

"Would you like to go eat? Isn't it time to eat?"—"I don't mind."—
"We don't have to. It's up to you." Gradually it switches gears; "I'm
famished . . . Nothing I ate could satisfy this hunger I'm having
right now." By the end, the person is talking about hunger that can
only subside briefly, but will return even stronger so that "there'll be
nothing left but the hunger itself when it comes back. Nothing left
but the hunger eating the hunger when it comes back."

Another section was triggered by a phone conversation Chaikin
had with his brother. Chaikin described to Shepard how this
brother had developed an oddly businesslike persona that he used
now even with his family—and how that image finally encroached
on the basically sensitive, socially conscious person who projected
it. Chaikin did an imitation of his brother, and Shepard said, "It's
wonderful. Let's put it in." They developed a spoken letter,
performed in a flat, dry tone. What communicated was a stifled,
hopeless attempt at caring and contact:

> I'm writing you this today from a very great distance. Everything
> here is fine. I'm hoping everything there is fine with you. I'm hoping
> you still miss me as much as you once did. . . .
>
> Something happened today which you might find amusing. I
> know I found it amusing at the time. A dog came into the hotel
> and ran around the lobby. . . .

Although they felt, in Shepard's words, "no urgency to tie these
facets [of the developing pieces] together or force them to tell a
'story,'" "Tongues" did wind up with a kind of double-yolked
center—not too far removed from the original story idea of the
man who dies. One repeating theme is voices, the total inadequacy
and the miraculous expressiveness of sounds, especially words.
Chaikin, as woman giving birth, in a mixture of agony and awe,
says, "Nothing they told me was like this. I don't know whose skin
this is." A character tries frantically to find a voice he can recognize
as his own, running through an orchestra of vocal timbres and
pitches in the search: "That was me. Just then. That was it. Me . . .
Must've been. Who else? Why should I doubt it?" And the final
segment is about really learning to hear:

> Today the people talked without speaking.
>   Tonight I can hear what they're saying.
>
> Today the tree bloomed without a word.
>   Tonight I'm learning its language.

Even more central is the theme of death and dying. This focus came partly from the original story idea, partly from Chaikin and Shepard's interest in expressing extreme conditions—and partly from the fact that Chaikin literally was in heart failure. (He underwent emergency open-heart surgery days after returning to New York):

> I was very sick when we were working on "Tongues," extremely sick, and I didn't know it. And I'd work with Sam and then I'd go back to the hotel room, unless we had never left the hotel room, and I'd lie and look at the ceiling. It was in a geriatric hotel; I wanted to be there because of the feeling that I wouldn't ever be old and I might as well just be around oldness on this occasion when I was out of town anyway.

"Tongues" circles back again and again to death. The opening is about a man who lives "in the middle of a people," is honored, dishonored, married, becomes old, and then one night dreams a voice telling him, "You are entirely dead . . . You are entirely gone from the people"—and "In the next second/He's entirely dead." The theme resurfaces later in a haunting litany:

> Between the space I'm leaving
> and the space I'm enjoying
>
> The dead one tells me now
>
> Beside the shape I'm leaving
> and the one I'm becoming
>
> The departed tells me now.

Another voice talks about the "moment where I vanished," leaving "the whole of my body." There is an address to a dead one who is somehow present: "Is this me calling you up/or are you appearing? Volunteering yourself?" And one section near the end is about comforting a dying person, trying to guess what comes at the moment of death.

Shaping the dozen-plus sections of "Tongues" into a performance piece, Chaikin and Shepard used principles drawn more from musical composition than traditional dramaturgy. Rather than looking for a story line, consistent characters, or an Aristotelian beginning, middle, and end, they worked with statement, development, and counterpoint. Although only one character/

mode actually repeats in the piece (the person trying to find his voice), themes from the various sections play off, orbit around and build onto one another. Chaikin, whose ensemble creations have mostly been constructed this way, says: "One of the things which we share, Sam and me, is our intense involvement with music. We're never looking for the dramatic structure. We're looking for [a] . . . shape that's musically tenable."

As the words of "Tongues" became more set, Shepard and Chaikin decided there should be some kind of instrumental accompaniment. The original conception for the piece had included music as an essential part, but they had forgotten about it. Chaikin rekindled the idea about a week before they were to start performing—partly, he claims, because of nervousness about being up on stage all alone: "I think actors are insecure anyway, but in my case I perform at these irregular intervals, so I'm insecure for those reasons as well. And I have so many opinions about acting, more and more and more. And here I am performing!"

He and Shepard each tried to telephone a musician (the two people who later performed "Tongues" and "Savage/Love" in New York). Then Shepard said he'd like to do the sounds himself; "I felt it would be terrific if we could both be in it." So, Chaikin recalls, laughing:

> Since Harry's line was busy and Skip wasn't home, rather than pursue it I said, "Terrific." And I thought 4/5 "terrific" and 1/5 "What if he does music like he sort of slaps against some guitar and thinks that's it?" And then it just was wonderful! Sam's a very good percussionist. He's not only musical as a writer.

Shepard brought a selection of instruments to the theatre (by now they were working in the Magic Theatre, where "Tongues" was first performed), and they started to jam and experiment. They devised a percussion accompaniment on traditional and invented instruments—bongos, cymbals, maracas, an African drum, a tambourine, bells, chains, pipes, brass bowls, kitchenware. The voice addressing the blind one was accompanied by the high, eerie whine of a brass bowl being vibrated by a soft mallet—a sound which suggested the noise of a mosquito. Seeds inside a long, thin drum pittered and rolled as the tube was rotated during the childbirth speech. A section about wanting to change from a job involving noisy, dangerous machinery was accented by the chains being smashed down against metal pipes. A rhythmic jingling of bells undercut the possible morbidity of the long series of guesses about "When you die . . ." The final section, about learning to hear, was said to the low, pastel gong of broiler trays.

Both men wanted to keep the focus on Chaikin while making the music an integral part of the performance. They had already decided that Chaikin would face front in a chair, motionless except for his head, his lap covered with a blanket. Now Shepard sat behind him, back to back, on a low platform, the instruments arranged around him. As he played he periodically held his arms and instruments out so that they could be seen over the top or around the sides of Chaikin's chair. For the opening section, about the man born in the middle of a people, an arm repeatedly reached to the side shaking maracas, punctuating the speech both visually and aurally; the brass bowl and mallet appeared later held on the other side of the chair; the tube with seeds was held high over Chaikin's head. Shepard invented and scored the various gestures (which, of course, neither he nor Chaikin could see) trying to give the sense that his arms, in motion, were "extensions of Joe's static body."

The total stage picture suggested illness and also, somehow, a priest or medium through whom voices come. Chaikin suspects, though, that the show's visual austereness was the result of medical as much as thematic considerations: "I think I furtively got Sam to agree that this would be interesting, even though we didn't want it to be like *Endgame* or something with this guy in a chair. I think I got him to do that because I had no other choice physically." But Shepard responded when told Chaikin's comment, "It wasn't hard to agree. We originally had said it would just be a voice piece. And that staging put the focus on Joe's voice and face—on that voice and amazing, expressive face."

Before Chaikin had even left San Francisco, he and Shepard were talking about doing another piece as soon as their schedules allowed. During the year, then, Chaikin made *Re-Arrangements* with his Winter Project workshop, and that piece became a kind of bridge between the two California works. It incorporated several sections of "Tongues"—and it moved into an area that neither he nor Shepard had dealt with much in their plays: love. Chaikin suggested that the second San Francisco collaboration continue exploring this theme and Shepard wrote back: "I've been wondering about a dialogue concerning love for over a year now, so it's almost uncanny that you suggest it. . . . I can hardly wait to start on this with you."

Although they had exchanged letters about the upcoming work, and Chaikin had suggested several books for Shepard to read (including Simone de Beauvoir's memoirs about her life with Sartre), they once again started their rehearsal period with no form or text. What they did have this time was a theme—and, more important, the experience of the first collaboration:

> Sam met me at the airport, and we dealt with the baggage—and then I said, "We've got three weeks!" We both said it was crazy. I said, "We haven't even begun." Sam said, "I know"—and then he said, "Yes, we have." And he was right.

Shepard explains:

> We had already established certain guidelines in working before. I have the feeling that this collaboration seemed to go much smoother in a way, in terms of being hooked up to each other so that we didn't have to go through a lot of unnecessary dialogue. The last time it was feeling out what would be a method of working together. And we discovered it. But this time was much more fluid.

The theme was a tricky one. First of all, collaboration involves coming together on shared ground—and, superficially at least, Chaikin and Shepard don't have a lot of common ground in their dealings with love. Shepard has a tight, extended nuclear family— wife, child, in-laws; Chaikin forms deep and lasting relationships, but not long-term, primary ones. Shepard is straight; Chaikin bisexual. They found, though—contrary to Chaikin's initial apprehensions—that it wasn't hard at all to find terrains of shared experience. Shepard was not surprised: "We were trying to deal with the interior of it. And it doesn't really matter what your exterior circumstances are in relationship to it, because the interior, I think, is where you find the common ground with anything."

The work process on "Savage/Love" was different than on "Tongues" in that, Chaikin explains, "it was a theatrical dialogue rather than conversation." Shepard describes their method:

> We would agree on a particle of the subject, sometimes very small things, and Joe would start to work as an actor, improvising around that particle. Sometimes the language that he used in the improvisation to investigate what the material was became the language of the script. I would take it down and rearrange it and mess with it a little, and then that became the actual text.

Shepard became more and more drawn to Chaikin's feeling for language:

> Joe has a poetic sense without using elaborate or fancy words, without being excessive. The language is stripped in a way that's ordinary, but the ordinariness serves as a kind of jolt. There's something undramatic about a line like "The first moment I saw you in the post office" that makes it have a dramatic impact.

Once again, the delineations of writer versus director broke down. Some sections are mostly Chaikin's words edited by Shepard; some are Shepard's words filtered through Chaikin.

The play came to focus less on the joys and ecstasy of love, though they're included, than on its pain. A recurring theme is the lover's paralyzing, tormenting self-consciousness—wondering what the desired one sees and how to shape a self that will be most lovable. A voice says, "When we're tangled up in sleep/Is it my leg you feel your leg against/Or is it Paul Newman's leg? . . . If you could only give me some clue/I could invent the one you'd have me be." In another part, the speaker strikes a pose and asks, "When I sit like this/Do you see me brave/ . . . Which presentation of myself/Would make you want to touch/What would make you cross the border." Another character watches himself in conversation, trying to make his face and body transmit what he wants them to, unable to make them cooperate.

Several times in "Savage/Love," Chaikin and Shepard use the image of killing—always metaphorically—to express both the hatred in love and what happens when passion dies. One speech, by someone who's just "killed" his partner, ends, "I saw you thinking of something else/You couldn't see/The thing I'd done to you." Another voice, a person watching a sleeping lover, says, "For one moment I think of the killing/ . . . I want to strangle your dreams/Inside me."

The most wrenching section of "Savage/Love," and one of the funniest, is a part Shepard and Chaikin call "The Beggar." They began by writing a monologue of somebody pleading for a crumb, moving from "Could you give me just a small part of yourself" to, finally, "Could I just walk behind you for a little while." When that speech was done, Shepard and Chaikin felt there also should be a part showing the reverse—so they created a monologue that began "Don't think I'm this way with everybody/ . . . In fact, usually it's the other way around" and, by the end, was "I'm wasting my time right now/Just talking to you." Shepard had the idea, then, to run the two speeches together as segments of one voice. "It seems to be true," he explains, "that one emotion is absolutely connected to its opposite, and the two sides are actually simultaneously happening. You can't show the simultaneousness of it so much, but you can show how they evolve—they don't really evolve, they just flip."

The bleakness of "Savage/Love" is undercut not only by its (relatively few) affirming voices, but especially by its humor. Lots of it is funny, even as it is painful: A lover tries out different terms of endearment to see which will fly; a character declares he's lost fifteen pounds and dyed his hair brown, all for a beloved he has yet to find. "One of the wonderful things about Sam," Chaikin says, "is that he's funny. There has to be a certain proportion of humor in everything he does. It's as clear as that there would have to be pepper on somebody's food or vegetables as part of a casserole. It's very important. Anything without humor at all is very hard to care about."

Because of the briefness of the work period, some areas that Chaikin and Shepard had meant to explore were not worked out. Chaikin told an interviewer:

> On my way to the airport I realized that we had not dealt with the terror of replaceability one can feel with love. Both of us wanted to include it, we both thought it was integral and even central to the whole thing, and it isn't there because we couldn't finish the piece together because we live on different coasts. (*New York Times*, January 13, 1980)

They were satisfied enough with what they had been able to do, though, to give the piece a firm shape. Once again, their approach was more musical than dramaturgical; they worked with shapes, rhythms, and thematic relationships, but did not try at all to mold their material into a story.

Instrumental music also became very important in the piece. "As we were writing," Shepard says, "we were really trying to think in terms of being economical enough with the words so that it left space where music could really make the environment for it." In program notes for the San Francisco production, he wrote, "Both of these collaborations are an attempt to find an equal expression between music and the actor."

Two musicians, Harry Mann, who had performed in several

Shepard works, and Skip LaPlante, who had been in Chaikin's Winter Project, collaborated on "Savage/Love." Mann played clarinet, sax, flute, and various whistles in the piece—often honky-tonking humor into Chaikin's monologue. The "I've lost fifteen pounds for you" speech, for instance, was counterpointed by a jazzy, syncopated alto sax. When Chaikin, looking placidly at the audience, began to wail a few bars of "The thrill is gone," Mann accentuated the irony by precisely matching his pitch, timing, and mood on the sax.

LaPlante (who also learned Shepard's accompaniment for "Tongues" and performed in the New York and European productions) used mostly homemade instruments constructed from trash—chains, metal strips, kitchenware, fluorescent tubes, wooden planks—as well as a double bass. During the "Beggar" section, he jangled chains in a wicker basket, making a sound vaguely like coins in a tin cup. For an angry, accusing speech—"YOU/who controls me/ . . . YOU/Who leads me to believe we're forever in love"—he used a homemade bull-roarer, a plank of wood whirled on a string to make a noise like a car motor. For a lover's recollection of "days by the water," he created a muted, glubby percussion by tapping the lid of a peanut butter jar partly filled with water.

Often Chaikin, Mann, and LaPlante played as a trio. While Chaikin spoke of being "haunted by your scent/When I'm talking to someone else," LaPlante made a hollow, eerie sound by bowing metal strips, and Mann created a high, quivering dissonance by blowing two penny whistles at once. For the "fifteen pounds" speech, LaPlante tapped a spunky rhythm on a kitchen bowl.

The physical staging this time was less austere but still extremely spare. Chaikin performed from a niche about four feet off the ground—six feet high, five feet wide, and two and a half feet deep. He sat, stood, lay down, and squirmed in his little space: once during the "Beggar," he even left it for a few moments to follow behind his loved one. The musicians, their instruments arranged around them, were further downstage to either side of Chaikin, visible yet funneling focus in to him. The lighting, designed by Beverly Emmons, was full of "specials"—in contrast to her design for "Tongues," which was subtly modulating white illumination. New voices were marked by light changes, sometimes as extreme as a tight spot from directly above or one side, which helped to punctuate the monologue and define its sections.

"Tongues" and "Savage/Love" opened at the Public Theater in

November 1979 to critical acclaim. Mel Gussow wrote about the program twice, first a daily review, then a long Sunday *New York Times* feature. He described the production as "not only an exquisite piece of performance theater," but also "to a great extent, a consolidation, a précis of the work of these two extraordinary theater artists over a span of fifteen years." James Leverett wrote in the *Soho News*, "What emerges is the pure presence of an extraordinary actor—mature, classic in its economy, consummate in its power." The *Village Voice* made my article on the collaboration the week's lead arts feature.

Both men also are pleased with their collaboration. In fact, they plan to create another theatre piece as soon as their schedules permit—definitely with music, probably with more physical movement (an area they had hoped to explore in "Savage/Love"), and maybe even with one or two actors. "I'd like to do a lot more with Joe," Shepard says: "I'd love to keep working with him over a long period of time." Chaikin agrees: "We don't know what's going to come of it, but we feel that there's a fertility."

-- 6 --

Working Notes
and Variants

The following abbreviations and symbols have been used:

[ ]	editor's notes.
/ /	text between brackets has been crossed out.
∧ ∧	text between marks has been inserted.
f	folio, used for unnumbered pages of notebooks.
r	recto
v	verso
p	page

Sam Shepard:
"Tongues" Notebook

(Notes begun 5/15/78—performed 6/7/78)
In collaboration with Joe Chaikin, Magic Theatre, San Francisco.

f2r

Song of Bone   (5/15/78)

STORY	SONG	CHANT
Cage of rib	. . .	Cage of heart
Bone	.	Home
In here	. .	In here
Bone	.	Home

Cage of rib	. . .	Cage of heart
Walk	.	Talk
In here	. .	In here
Talking	. .	Moaning
Cage of Bone	. . .	Cage of blood
Song	.	Song
Song of bone	. . .	Song alone
Song	.	Song
Sing bone / Song of/	. . .	Singing Bone
Ring	.	Sing
In here ringing	. . . .	In here singing
Talk me heart	. . .	Sing me heart
Song	.	Long
In here beating	. . . .	To me healing
Sing	.	Sing
Long	.	Long
In here song	. . .	Sing me song
Gone	.	Come
Long time waiting	. . . .	No more waiting

f2v

From the hotel
To the beach

From the beach
To the café

From the café
To the truck

From the truck
To the beach

From the beach
To the park

From the park
To the sidewalk

From the sidewalk
To the people

From all these people
To us

From us
To each other

From each other
To ourselves

Apart
Together
Apart

f3r

If I could be saved by a word
If I could be saved by the sun
If I could be saved

If I could be saved by a voice
By a tongue
By a single break in the noise
By a song
I could be saved

If I could be saved by a name
By a gun
By a worship
A prayer
By a God of nowhere
I could be saved

If I could be saved by a man
By a / boy / grin
By a girl
I could be saved
By a girl

If I could be saved by a look
By a glance
By a dog
By a beast from the sky

f3v

If I could be saved by a rain
By a cloud
If all hoping was gone
All wishing
All hunger
All aching
Was gone

If I could be saved by a grin
I'd be taken away

If I could be saved
I'd depart

If I could be saved
I'd be gone

If I could be saved

f4r

If the voice were a mask would it look the same as it sounds?

Story of rebirth

Chair—tied to character
Skin

Hotel Carlton
Sutton and Larkin

f5r

Story: (5/16/78)   [only major variants listed]
He was born in the middle of a story which he had nothing
   to do with.
In the middle of a tribe
In the middle of a people who are the whole world.
And he never leaves.

Stanza 7:
He played with leaves
He became a boy
He played with games
He became a man
He played with life
He was honored, etc.

f6r

Stanza 9:
A voice
A voice comes
In his dream
A voice comes
A voice he has never heard

[NOTE: Throughout this version "tribe" is generally used when "people" occurs in the final version.]

f6v

Breath—brings a voice   *interlude*
Breath—brings this voice:
Worker
Voice: If I get this job, etc., as in final version except for last unit which reads:
Pay's just as good. Get the same insurance. That other job—that other job

Voice: Everybody tried to prepare me.
         [Continues to f7r as in final text with minor variant.]

f8r

Chant—Song   5/17

Ocean sounds
By itself
/Sand fall/ Water moans
By itself
Giant water
By itself

From itself
/This/ Big water
Pushing
By itself

From its own
This motion
Giant
Crashing

By itself
This moaning
Heard
In me

Just the same
From itself
Volcanic
Rushing
On its own

f8v

By itself
Green water
Running

f9r

Story of the turtles being eaten by the birds who get sick from the turtles and die and then are eaten by dogs who die and are in turn eaten by vultures.

Story of worm cut in half—each half fights the other half—each half is cut in half and each half keeps fighting the other half—Kierkegaard

Trance Voice—voice that interrupts it
Repeated Moment—cycle
Voice calling for the *voice* it recognizes as itself

Where was it—where is it—this—is this it—let's see—how does this sound—is this the sound of me—my sound—

Secret Voice—the Perfect Interview (two voices)—exclusive interview

Companion Voice—depicting world to Blind One—color, shapes, texture—

f9v

A *word* that becomes broken into sound

"Hunger"—

Rocking voice—(from dead)—*keening*

Song to the Skin
   (renewal)

Dialogue to the Body

Talking letter
   I'm writing this from a very great distance

f10r

Trance Voices (Voices of Hunger)   5/19
[through fllv. variant in final section as follows:]

I'm always hungry.

I'm so hungry I could eat a horse! My hunger knows no bounds! Nothing I ate could satisfy this hunger. This hunger. This hunger eats me it's so hungry. This hunger is eating me alive.

   (talking "Hunger" into sound each time it's used)

f12r

                                    5/19

Song of Skin

   To this skin
   To which I've grown accustomed
   To this covering

To this sky
Which blankets me
In day or nite
To this old skin
which dies and grows
/Without my knowing/ how/ In secret invisible/

To bodies yet unfolded

f13r

Invocation to a *Dead Voice*

/ In a secret part of the air
the dead ones gather

Someone tells me now

/In/Between the fall of the hand
the turn of the head

Someone tells me now/

Between the face I'm making
and the face that's coming

5

Someone tells me now

Between the ear and
the air it swallows

4

Someone tells me now

Beside the shape I'm leaving
and the one I'm becoming

3

Someone tells me now

Between the breath I'm breathing
and the one that's coming

1

Someone tells me now

f13v

Behind the voice that's speaking
   and the one that's thinking   ⎤
                                                  ⎥ 6
Someone tells me now   ⎦

Between the space I'm leaving
   and the space I'm joining   ⎤
                                                  ⎥ 2
Someone tells me now   ⎦

f14r

Voice from the Dead
   There was this moment. I saw it coming. I could see it
coming toward me. There was this moment just ahead. I tried
to keep myself from crashing into this moment. I tried to go
around it. I tried to freeze it. I tried to pull away. I even told
myself this moment didn't exist. Nothing I did could stop this
collision from taking place. This crash between me and the
moment of my death.

f15r

Inquisition of Dead One
[variant ending begins after "What are you asking?"]
I see you in some other way.

f15v

Is it you or me only seeing
   you through my own longing?

f16r/v

Talking Letter
[minor variants; ends with "Respectfully, Michael Lewis Scott"]

f18r

Voice to One About to Die
[paragraph as in final text]
When you *die*/you go straight to
   Heaven or Hell
When you *die*/you disintegrate
   into energy.

When you *die*/you're reborn
    into another body
When you *die*/you turn to
    shit.
When you *die*/you travel to
    other planets.
When you *die*/you die forever.
When you *die*/you never come
    back.
When you *die*/it's absolutely final.
∧   When you die
    you die.   ∧
When you die
    you get to start all over

f18v

When you die
    you get marked in the book.
When you die
    You're rejoined with your ancestors.
When you die
    All your dreams will come true.
When you die
    You speak to the angels.
When you die
    you'll get what you deserve.

f19r

Talk Song
Today the wind roared through the center of town.
Tonight I hear its voice.
Today the river lay wide open to the sun.
Tonight I hear it speaking.
Today the moon remained in the sky.
Tonight I feel it talking.
Today the people talked without speaking.
Tonight I can hear what they're saying.
Today the tree bloomed without a word.
Tonight I'm learning its language.

f20r

/ *Speechless*/ /*Pompous Voice*

It's not often, actually, that I find myself at a loss for words. But in this particular instance I found myself speechless. Absolutely numb. No words could even begin to describe the impact of it. The total emancipation of one's personal rhetoric was indeed awesome.

Leader's Voice

I'm not here today to lay down the law to you people. On the contrary. I'm not here so that you can openly voice your opinions. I'm here so that you can see that those opinions are not falling on deaf ears. I'm here so that we can join together in this struggle. So that we can unite. Which has haunted us for more than a decade.

f21r

Story of Myself

When you listen to me
  is it me you're hearing?
Is it you I'm hearing
  when you answer to me?
Am I talking to the one
  I imagine you to be?
Are you speaking to
  the imagined one in me?

Am I telling the story of myself
  to myself, while I'm
  hearing the story of you?

Who is it you're telling your story to?

f22r

Tongue

Well, actually, I have no regrets. Not really. Well maybe one or two things. / Can't do much about now. / You know, stupid, little things. Just things that sort of stick in your memory. You know, like saying the wrong thing to the wrong person at the wrong time. Things like that. Just little things.

Maybe one or two wrong decisions. That's all. Just one or two. Nothing catastrophic. Nothing that couldn't be fixed up later.

Well, actually, there was this one thing—just this one. There was this one thing that I wish— / But there's nothing I can do about that now. I can't go back and change that now.

f22v

That's already happened. I wish it hadn't happened but it did happen. If it wasn't for that one thing—If it wasn't for that then everything would've been perfect. /—hadn't happened the way it happened. I mean I guess it had to happen the way it happened but I still wish it hadn't.

f23r

Second Voice to Blind One
In front of you is the moon.

f23v

The thoughts about one's death are emanating from the idea of who I am. When I'm afraid of my death it's the "I" that's afraid. Is there another "I" which sees this "I" that's afraid and in seeing this "I" that's afraid begins to understand its fears? When "I'm" afraid of dying I'm afraid of losing this "I" which is afraid. The fear is a ramification of this "I" trying to hold onto its life. Another "I" which sees the "I" that's afraid also sees that this "I" that's afraid is totally illusory. That it doesn't in fact exist. It has no tangible body, only an idea of itself which it desperately wants to cling onto (preserve).

f24r

> *Shakers*
> (*Story*)—
> *Bongos* to *Doumbak*
> (*Worker*)—single steel
> *African shake drum*
> (*New Mother*)
> *Jam*
> ("*Where—Let's see—*")
> *Fade tempo*
> (*Blind*)—Gong

(Hunger)—*Scraper Gourd*
   Bells
("Between breath")
   Wood block—*time*
("There was this moment")—*fade*
   Cowbell—*pulse*
("Is this you in death?")
   Cowbell talks—seven—into
("I—There—I. Me.")—*Short Jam*
("Song")—*Cymbal*—*straight time*
("Letter")—*Cymbal*—*single strokes*
   Doumbak
("Pompous—Leader")
("When you die")—*Bells*—shake
   Talk Song—

f29r

What is performance? The act of performance. It seems that performance can only be understood in relationship to an audience. The witnessing of the performer performing. The actor and the character are not the same thing and this distinction is what the audience recognizes immediately. As the performance continues, the audience may lose track of this original impression and drift into the dream that the actor actually is the character. Later, after the play, the audience may remark on what a remarkable performance the actor gave. "I actually believed he was the character."

"Tongues": First Typed Draft, Shepard Copy

[Revisions and music notes in pencil by Shepard]
Cover Page
Tongues Magic Theatre, S.F. [handwritten]
Scene: A straight-backed chair draped with a Mexican blanket, extreme downstage center. Directly behind the chair on a low riser are various percussion instruments. The lights go to black and come back up to reveal a man sitting in the chair with the blanket now draped over his lap, concealing his body from the waist down. As he begins to speak, the arms of the percussionist, whose body is hidden behind the chair, become visible at different moments throughout the piece as he plays the various instruments in accompaniment to the speaker. The speaker's body remains completely motionless except for his neck and head throughout the piece.

NOTE: This piece was originated through collaboration and therefore the choices arrived at for the production were extremely personal and inseparable from the people and conditions of that time.

1st Draft   needs revision   no music notations [handwritten]

p. 1

Story

He was born in the middle of a story which he had nothing to do with.
/ In the middle of a tribe /
In the middle of a people

In the middle of a people he stays

p. 2

[Continues as in notebook version. Handwritten changes include: changing the refrain "Are in the tribe" to "Are with the people"; deleting the line "All his love" from stanza 3; changing "tribe" to "people" in stanza 6, line 1; deleting the first five lines from stanza 7; and changing stanza 9 to read as in final version.]

The four lines beginning, "You are entirely dead," are labeled ("Dream Voice":) and the heading (*Story contd.*) is written in after them.

p. 3

(*Breath*—Interlude—breathing brings a voice)

("Worker's Voice")
[Text as in final version]

("Imagined Interview with Secret Voice")

Let me ask you just this one thing since it's so rare we get a chance to talk to you. In all of your myriad travels, where is it you find the food to be the most exceptional?

The food?

Yes.

I don't think that's a pertinent question, to tell you the truth.

Well, let me put it this way. Since this is a rare opportunity we certainly don't want to waste it on trivial questions.

No.

What is your view on the question of death and re-birth?

[This whole sequence is deleted by hand.]

p. 4

("New Mother's Voice")
[Text as in final version]

("Voice Calling for the Recognized Voice")

Where—Let's see—Is this, etc. [as in final version]

p. 5

("Voice to the Blind One")

[Text as in final text up to "A car goes by," then:]
Moths are plunging into the glass trying to get at the light
from the lamp. Tiny bugs crawl. The electricity fades, then
comes back. / A cobweb billows up from a light breeze. / You
can feel the breeze through the room. The same breeze you
feel is moving the smoke through the room. Your cigarette
burning. Everything else is still. Absolutely still. Nothing is
moving now except for your breathing. Your chest. The shirt
on your chest. The shirt you're wearing is blue. Your glasses
are black. / As black as night. / Your glasses reflect the image
of you from the glass of the window. A mosquito races around
your ear. The same mosquito you're hearing.

p. 7

("Voices of Hunger")

[Text as in final text with minor variants. Ends as follows:]
When it comes back there'll be nothing left but the hunger
itself when it comes back. Nothing left but the hunger itself.
Nothing left but the hunger. Nothing left but the hunger

eating the hunger. Nothing left but the hunger eating itself. Nothing left but the hunger. The hunger.
The hunger.
The hunger
The hunger.
(Repeats until it disappears.)

[The last series of "The hunger" are deleted.]

("Invocation to a Voice from the Dead")

[Revises notebook version to final text.]

p. 8

("Voice from the Dead")

[First paragraph is text from notebook and is deleted by hand, leaving final three paragraphs as in final text.]

p. 9

("Inquiry to the Dead One")

[No variants.]

p. 10

("Voice Calling for the Recognized Voice")

I—There—I. Me. Me saying "I" to myself. That was me. Just then. That was it. Me. I speak. Me. No one else. That was me just then. Must've been. Who else? Why should I doubt it? Not me? Who else could it have been? / Something still uncertain. Something still up in the air. Why should that be? Why should that be the case? Why shouldn't this still be

the same one as the one just before this? The same one
continuously. The same one forever. Why not just call it me
anyway? Even with doubt. Just for the sake of reconciliation.
For the sake of making a truce. No. That's not what I mean
to say. Nothing remotely like it. What I mean to say—I can't
hear myself saying it! that's the problem. That's part of the
problem. I can't recognize this voice now. This one right now.
It's like me but it isn't. It's sort of like me but not really. Not
the whole picture. Not totally how I picture my voice to myself.
How I picture me telling myself. The story of myself. Heard
only by others. No. Heard never by me? No. Heard occasionally
by me and always by others? No. Heard never by neither one
of us? No. Never. Always heard from above? No. Maybe? No.
Maybe yes, maybe no. Heard and always understood from on
high? No. Absolutely not. Can't convince me of that. Not on
your life. Then who then? Who then what? *Who is it that hears
me?* When? *Now!* nothing. *No one?* Never. *Can't be!* maybe.
Never! I'm not convinced. I'm not convinced I'm not the same
one always and forever. I'm not convinced I'm not heard in
a certain kind of way. Uniquely my own. Unmistakably me
and no other. Even if I can't hear it someone else must.
Someone else has to! /
[Beside this cut passage is written "Song?" Following it written
into the text is "*Sings*: from this moment on—you and me
dear—only two for tea dear—from this moment on—(repeats
in prolonged tones)"]

("Talking Letter")

[No variants.]

p. 11

("Talk Song")

[Version as in notebook but typed in couplets. Line 6 revised
to final form: "Tonight I/hear/feel it/talking/moving." This
unit is circled and "end" is written in the margin.]

p. 12

("Pompous Voice")

[Revised to final form; changes handwritten.]

("Leader's Voice")

[No variants.]

("Voice to One About to Die")

[No variants.]

p. 13

("Story of Myself")

[As in notebook. Deleted in pencil.]

("Voice to the Blind One")

In front of you is the moon. [Deleted in pencil.]

Sam Shepard:
"Savage/Love" Notebook

Notes—Text
SAVAGE/LOVE
notes and text
Eureka Theatre, San Fran.
8/79
performed 9/5/79
collaboration with Joe Chaikin
Skip LaPlante—percussion, bass
Harry Mann—alto sax, woodwinds

f2r

Savage Love   8/79
Joe—August Notes

how need for another comes from emptiness—the need to be
   filled
gestures of open and closedness
—receiving, denying
   The Ghost of Love
   Modes of Love:
   Varieties of Love
Love as attraction—(magnetic, unconscious, the subject doesn't
know the source of its attraction)
Influence—a third force between two parties
Love as a Ghost
Love as the keeper of souls
Love as the understanding of another's mortality—the "seeing"
into another's lack of permanence

Love as nostalgia for a lost life or a life hoped for—a sense of
mystery
Narcissism
Love of the body (sexual love)

f2v

Love of myself in the past—"when I was like I wish I was
now"
Love of myself in the future—
Love as salvation from loneliness

f3r

Savage Love
Signs of Love   *Dummy Corpse*

Exiled
Beggar—Fool
Hunter
expectation of other

Crime of passion
The double
gestures of moving toward object of love and moving away
Thru the body   "It was by the breakwater"
The shock of loss   "The question is, who's paying for it"
The absence of the   "And then he gets to take her in the
other   back room and fuck her"
Couldn't speak   "And I watched your face become a
                     mask"
Nausea   The Hoax of Love
Stanza of movements from closed to open—music and body only
Replaceable
Acting Out
Waiting for the you to appear
Hellos and good-byes
/ Beginnings and Endings /
Terms of Endearment

f4r

> *Eureka Theatre—S.F.*   8/16/79
> *Savage Love*
> [Through 5r this text is same as the piece called "Opening."]

f5v

"Tangled Up"

[The text is of the second of the pieces called "Killing" with no variants.]

f6r

I remember jumping up at one thing you said
But now I forget what it was

When people saw us in public
They couldn't know
/ They couldn't read /   "Killing"
It was in one moment
When we looked
When we saw each other
/ In one moment /   ˙
/ In / that / moment / I killed you

I saw you lying there
Unmourned

You didn't know
I didn't say ^   the thing I saw ^
 ^ I saw you thinking of something else ^
You couldn't see
 / what / ^   the thing ^   I'd done to you ^
Then
Leaving
You said something about leaving
we were hardly together
I thought I heard you
/ I thought I heard you say /

I thought I heard you saying
Something about forever
Was this forever
?—Even while I saw you dead
Were you saying
What I thought I heard you saying

f6v

∧ 2 ∧   When we're tangled up in meeting other people
Is it me you're introducing
Or is it Warren Beatty
   Raquel Welch
   Romeo and Juliet
   Marlon Brando
   Camille
   Casanova
   Don Juan
   Frank Sinatra
   Mick Jagger
[Added in margin at left and bottom of names]
∧ 5 ∧   When we're tangled up in love
   Is it me you're loving or another
∧ 3 ∧   When I move my eyes like this
   Is it causing you to think of Marlon Brando
∧ 6 ∧   If you could only give me some clue
   I could invent the one you'd have me be
∧ 4 ∧   When I stand with my body facing one direction
   And my head in the other
   Do you think of Jeanne Moreau

f7r

∧ 1 ∧   When we're tangled up in sleep
   Is it my leg you feel your leg against
   Or is it Paul Newman's leg

   / Maybe I live in your mind
   In a way that I'm not

   Maybe I live for you
   As the one who has fun

Maybe I live for you
As the protector/

[Following through to 8r is the text of "Watching the Sleeping
Lover" with variants as follows:]

Stanza 5:
I'm not very far from sleep
Your dream changes
To something else
You move
I breathe with you

Stanza 8 ends:
I feel sorry for the act

Stanza 10:
As the light comes thru
And nite is turning into day
I want to die before you
I want to die before we
Aren't lovers anymore

f8r

"Salvation"

Now that I'm with you I'm saved
    From all grief
Now that I'm with you I'm saved
    From being in parts
Now _____
    From hoping for anything else
Now _____
    From all other wanting

f9r

"Hoax"

variant line 3 crossed out:
Even tho this feels eternal

("Contempt")—Savage
You who makes me believe that we're lovers
You—my accomplice
You—who reminds me of myself
You—who lets me pretend
You—who controls me
You—who / allows / tells me to lie
You—who is acting as tho we're still in the first moment
You—who leads me to believe
    / that / we're forever in love

f10r

"Absence"

[2nd stanza deleted:]

Instead of blood
Something else is moving   rancid moves

My groin is locked

Your absence
The lack of you
Has / filled me up / taken over

f10v

"Haunted"

I'm haunted by your scent
When I'm talking to some/body / one else

I'm haunted by your eyes
In the middle of brushing my teeth

I'm haunted by your hair
By your scent
When you're not around

Are you visiting me
/ Even when you're not here /

Am I conjuring you up

f11r

"Listening Faces"

Stanza 5:
You told me secrets about / ones / people
    in your life who were strangers
    / in mine / to / me / mine.

Stanza 7:
You played me your music
/ I listened to the music you played me /
I couldn't hear the music in it

f11v

"How I Look to You"

[Second couplet added in margin. End as follows:]
Which presentation of myself

Would make you want to touch
Would you be more likely to touch
   if I signed you pretending I wasn't
Which signal would dissolve the talking
   to touching

f12r

"Beggar"—Inside/Outside

On the outside
I was wanting to give you the impression
Of a kind of certainty
A kind of weight

Tilt to one side
Tilt to the other

On the inside
the Beggar
(fragments—sound, words, music)

f13r

When I see you dead
My love aches for you alive

When I see you living
With no notion of it ending
My heart breaks for you alive

When I see us both gone
Two
Instead of one
This love is passing
To the living
This love is living

As we're gone
Suddenly I know I'm alone
Suddenly I know you can't save me
Suddenly I wish you were here

f14r

/"Acting"/

I'm not chasing you
I'm not parading myself
I'm not even expecting a return
But if only you could recognize me once
We could be whole

I'm not making myself different for you
I'm not putting on a mask
I'm not even / wanting / expecting a return
But if only you would open to me
We could both be transformed

"Acting Out"

[Variants begin with line ten:]
Now I watch you leaving / me /
Now I see you in anguish
/ While I'm feeling nothing /
Now I feel nothing

Now it's descended
It's come into my blood
I see the connection dissolving
Now it's as though we never knew each other
I see you getting in the taxi
I see you not talking to the driver
I see you hunting for a job and a new lover
I see you alone

f15r

"The Hunt"

[First line in final stanza crossed out:]
I've had my skin stretched for you

f16r

Songs

["The thrill is gone" as in final text.
Melody line of "I'm in the mood for love."]
"Fly Me to the Moon"
"Black Magic"

f17r

"First Moment"

[as in final text up to last two stanzas]

f18r
I felt something dissolving
I felt it might be dangerous

But anything could happen in the next moment
Maybe you would say anything
Or you could say you wanted to step out of your life
And let's go together forever

f19r

"Beggar" (with bowl)
[minor changes]

f21r

"Babble"

I wanna show how
∧ I ∧
I wanna show something tender
∧ Uh ∧
That uh—
Comes from you
But uh—
∧ My words ∧
I
Can't
∧ Find ∧
I wanna
Bring something out
that
some
but
It doesn't fit this time

f22r

Beginning
First moment
How I Look to You
Listening Faces
Babble
Killing
Hunt

f23r

Middle
Tangled Up
Opening

Salvation
Beggar
Savage
Killing(B)
Acting
Hoax
Haunted

f24r

End
Sleeping Lover
Absence
/ Beggar /

f25r

/*Signs of Love*/ ∧   *Savage Love* ∧   —(order)
First Moment
Listening Faces
Tangled Up
Babble (4)
∧   Terms of Endearment ∧
Killing—A
How I Look to You (3)
Beggar
Haunted
Savage
Acting
Absence
The Hunt
Killing—B
Watching Sleeping Lover
Salvation
∧   Babble (2) ∧
Hoax
Opening

f26r

"Terms of Endearment"

[as in final text]

f27r
"Babble (2)"
[as in final text]

Joseph Chaikin: Notes for the Cambridge Workshop

f1r

Introduction

All these pieces that follow are separated on the page by rules in between. They are to separate the sections. Each section is thought of as a song, or duet, or trio, or quartet—the words to be moved around in the most evocative, yet precise way that is found.

Sleep is the metaphor for states of being (identifiable or imaginary). The piece is moving through different sleeps. Sleeps having different rhythms, tempos, dynamics. It is not predictable what changes/moves the sleep. Frequently the music, sometimes the voice anticipating, sometimes the breathing.

The sleep condition will, I hope, permit a journeying that would include political and worldly parts as well as abstract and passionate movements.

The audience is included throughout in some way. The reason I have suggested that it be an indirect way is for the people working on it to search ways that are easy and not pressing, rather than ways that are coercive or embarrassing or making assumptions which are not shared. This contact with the audience is a delicate study that would go on throughout the embodying of this piece.

f2r

Through all the night
I waited
for the fighting to stop

The fighting
The battle roared with cursing and praying and killing

Prayers and killing
at the same time
All the night

They cried for everyone to pick up weapons
Take up arms
Clear
cries outside the window
Desperate
   voices outside my window
final shouting outside my/the window
loud shouting among the praying and cursing to take up arms

/ Human pattern
the fighting /
I told myself
I told her
fighting since the beginning
same fighting
different reasons
same killing
different places
same praying

No one to hold
nothing to hold onto
during the night
during the trance killing
during the trance killing

f3r

Between two thoughts
two poles

Come with me
Come along with me
/Drop (your   shoulders   and) ∧ do not say ∧
Drop
Drop
Moving now /
Somewhere in a sleep

so sharp
and clear
as eyes

Let it weep
if it does
weep
and clear
/ while /
during the while

---

or not at all

---

with the audience sitting
a moment

Always some ∧ where an ∧ audience
Always some sitting
Always

---

f4r

/ Standing in the middle of a room
turning round and round
one foot stays in the same place
the other foot makes a circle
turning round and round /

---

p. 1

Only once
Once
Only once
did everything shift so much

∧ Today ∧ I didn't want what I had always wanted
∧ When I woke up ∧
Not that I had always wanted the same things
in the same ways

But still there were return points
Points
Places
return places   points
again and again
wanting
returning

A moment
some moments   time moved (need to be reworded)

---

the earth
on the earth
confined to earth

---

not in the mind
not by the mind
not in that way

p. 2

/ Sometimes I sat and waited in a sitting position
Sometimes I was completely absorbed when standing. /

Where is the center   (about being lost)
my Love
Where is the center   my Love   ʌ   to be musicalized ʌ
Since I know which way is north, it would seem that I would
   know the center

I left my heart in San Francisco   (maybe some of the tune)
I left my head in Manhattan
I left my wallet in Paris
I left my soul by the water
   right next to the water
(this might be a "theme," returning what was left where)
(at some point maybe around of By the waters of Babylon)

Give me air
Give me air
Give me air

Let me loose
my friends, my lovers
let me loose

I broke into pieces
around the Mediterranean

---

p. 3

I'm going to sleep now
Now I am asleep
In this sleep
(My feet are dry
My fingers are cooler)
I don't see you anymore
only the walls inside my head
and pictures on different sides
Sometimes pictures of you
running away or toward
(Sometimes pictures of a neighbor's house when I was a child)
And all the while I can talk at the same time
Even   indistinctly   I   can sense you   actual

Now I move to another sleep
while the music changes
Moving
Just as the earth turns
and tilts toward the sun
and the sun is turning cool
My Love
Let me hold you in this sleep
You hold me
The sun is becoming cool   ^   cold?   ^

The dead say:
The stars are off their course
The constellations are splitting off
and out
Out

From the Cambridge Workshop

p. 1

Questions: "What's It Like Where You Come From?"

What's it like there?
Is it heaven? Do you live in heaven?

Where, exactly, do you come from?
Where in space?
How far away is it?
How would we locate it?

Is there night?
Is there day?
What's the light like there?
Are there seasons?
Is there time?
Do you see other galaxies?

Do you travel? Do you visit other stars? Other worlds?
Is there a limit to space?
What is the limit?

Is there music?
Are there trumpets?
Chariots?
Animals?
Is there silver and gold?

p. 2

"What's It Like"—contd.

Are there sexes? Different genders?
Do you have children?
Families?
Is there a hierarchy of Angels?
Where do you fit in the hierarchy?

Is there crime? Do you have rules and laws?
Betrayal? Do angels betray each other?
Do you fight with each other?
Are you loving?
How do you recognize Love?

Do you sleep?
Do you dream?
What do you eat?
Are you fond of meat?

Is your body like ours?
Do you ever get sick?
Is there disease where you come from?

Is there fire? Water? Land?
Do you have anything like furniture?
Do you have different temperatures?

p. 3

"What's It Like"—contd.

Do you dance?
Do you fall in love?
Do you touch each other?
Do you have taboos?

What do you fear most?

Are there other ones like you?
How many are there?

[Various speeches, each on a separate, unnumbered, page.]

ANGEL: There was a time when I felt I had a destination. I was moving toward something I thought I understood. There was an order that was clear to me. A lawful order. Then we were invaded. All the domains were shattered. The connections were broken. We were sent in a thousand directions. I'd be on a mission and forget where I was going. I'd try to return and forget how to find my way back. I'd be lost in between. That's how I crashed. In a moment of doubt—I crashed to earth.

SHE: I'm in a curious situation here. I don't belong to anybody or anything. I'm completely alone. Completely cut off. I live on these streets. They call me "Homeless." I'm a part of the "Homeless." That's the title they give you when you don't belong to anything or anyone. "Homeless." No one needs me and I don't need anyone. Including you.

SHE: I know lots of crazy people in this town, although I myself am not insane. I've saved myself from that. I know all kinds who think they're somebody else. They talk a blue streak. Can't stop talking—even if no one's there. They believe they're somebody else when they're not. Somebody important—like Mary Magdalene. Or John the Baptist. People like that. One guy thinks he's Ronald Reagan and he doesn't even care that Reagan's alive. I don't understand that. I had a cousin who thought he was controlling the moon. He wasn't. You think you're an Angel, but you could be just like my cousin. You could be totally deluded. Do you have any doubts that you're an Angel? Because if you don't, there's a good chance you're just kidding yourself. You can't kid me, though. I can tell right off when someone's pulling my leg. I have certain ways of knowing. Certain signs. I'll be testing you as we go along but you won't even know it.

SHE: If you can't speak or you won't speak, would you maybe
   sing? Can you sing? Aren't angels supposed to be in choirs
   and stuff? I love to sing, myself. Sometimes I sing for
   hours by myself. It keeps me company. I sing all kinds of
   songs. Songs I remember. Sometimes just pieces—little
   snatches I remember. Other times I make up stuff. Like
   here's one I made up. Do you want to hear it? Open your
   ears. Tell me what you think. It goes like this:
   ("I ain't got nobody
   Nobody's got me. . . .")

Bibliography

Manuscripts

Joseph Chaikin Papers. Department of Special Collections, Kent State University Library. Shepard letters. Cambridge Workshop texts. Chaikin Clipping files.

Joseph Chaikin Personal Files. Cambridge Workshop notes and fragments.

Sam Shepard Papers. Department of Special Collections, Mugar Memorial Library, Boston University. Chaikin letters. "Tongues" and "Savage/Love" notebooks and manuscripts.

Archives. New York Shakespeare Festival, Public Theatre. Promptscript and press clippings.

Videotape and Film

"Tongues." Videotape. San Francisco, 1978. American Poetry Archive, San Francisco.

"Tongues" and "Savage/Love." New York, 1979. Videotape of the New York Shakespeare Festival Production at the Public Theatre for the Theatre on Film and Tape Collection of the New York Public Library, Lincoln Center, New York.

"Tongues" and "Savage/Love." New York, 1980. Experimental video by Shirley Clarke.

Joseph Chaikin: Going On. Film by Steven Gomer, 1983.

Books

Auerbach, Doris. *Sam Shepard, Arthur Kopit and the Off Broadway Theatre.* Boston: Twayne, 1982.

Blumenthal, Eileen. *Joseph Chaikin: Exploring at the Boundaries of Theatre*. New York: Cambridge Univ. Press, 1984.

Chaikin, Joseph. *The Presence of the Actor*. Boston: Atheneum, 1972.

Marranca, Bonnie, ed. *American Dreams: The Imagination of Sam Shepard*. New York: PAJ, 1981.

Mottram, Ron. *Inner Landscapes: The Theatre of Sam Shepard*. Columbia, Missouri: Univ. of Missouri Press, 1984.

Poland, Albert, and Bruce Mailman. *The Off Off Broadway Book: The Plays, People, Theatre*. New York: Bobbs-Merrill, 1972.

Shepard, Sam. *Seven Plays*. New York: Bantam, 1981.

Shewey, Don. *Sam Shepard*. New York: Dell, 1986.

Afterword for the 2nd Edition

It is now ten years from the date when Joe Chaikin suffered a stroke. This book was one of the many projects that were part of Chaikin's recovery process, and it concludes with one of the most important early steps in that recovery, "The War in Heaven." Since completing that work, Chaikin and Shepard have continued to talk about working together. But it was only this past November that they were able to begin a new work, which is scheduled to be premiered in Atlanta in 1995.

For me what is vital in this book is the artistic concerns of both Chaikin and Shepard: the series of questions they addressed as they created the texts. It is my hope that bringing together the traces of the Chaikin/Shepard collaborations will inspire performers to take the journey demanded by these texts.

In the program note to the New York Shakespeare Festival production of "Tongues," Shepard wrote, "Both these collaborations are an attempt to find an equal expression between music and the actor. They are like environments where words and gestures are given temporary atmospheres to breathe through sound and rhythm." This interestingly represents the writer's position as: What is found between the music and the actor is the word. Shepard, writing to Chaikin a year before the work on "Tongues" began, noted he was "still obsessed with this idea that words are pictures and that even momentarily they can wrap the listener up in a visual world without having to commit themselves to revealing any other meaning. The sounds and rhythms seem to support these images and bring feeling into it."

If Shepard was searching for a word that, like music, could transcend literal meaning, Chaikin was working from the actor to give language an expressiveness he felt it had lost. In an interview Chaikin explained that, "The work I was doing asked of the actor another kind of use of the voice. It wasn't simply to have a nice voice, the kind of radio-announcer voice that actors often go after. But rather to have *other voices*, other voices drawn from *other selves* within the actor." He noted, "The spoken word is too often simply giving sound to the printed word. We should want to find how to speak words, not simply as data, but using sounds which make up the word to create the universe of the word."

The relationships actor-text, text-music, voice-music, character-voice, actor-character are central to the work created by Chaikin and Shepard. If performers are to bring these texts to life, it is important that they approach them in the spirit of Chaikin and Shepard themselves. Each performer or group working on these texts must regard rehearsal and performance as a rich process that involves delving into self and finding support in the rhythm of language and the interaction with music. There is not one right way to perform this work: each new production should find its own solutions and be an original response to its situation and performers.

One example of a way to work on the texts in this book was a student production, *The Chaikin/Shepard Project*, produced at Kent State University to coincide with the book's original publication in 1989. The company was made up of five actors, a guitarist and a percussionist. The production was staged by Alan Benson, à faculty director, and I served as dramaturg.

During the rehearsal process a four-part structure for the evening gradually emerged. The first section, "Voices: A Collage," was made up of the eight "voice" pieces from "Tongues," two monologues from the Cambridge Workshop, and five texts from the *Nightwalk* material. The actors worked without music, focusing on the creation of character through the voice and the rhythm of the language. "Talk Song" from "Tongues" was used to conclude this section. The second section was made up of "Savage/Love," performed as written. The major difference between this and the original production was the use of rock music rather than jazz, which seemed a natural choice for a student production.

After an intermission, the third section, "When You Die," brought together the pieces from "Tongues" that involved chant and invocation. The percussionist followed Shepard's notes to the published text to create the musical environment. Here the actors worked with the rhythms and with a language that was not tied to specific characterization. The final section, "Captured Angel," started with the Guard's questions to the Angel from the Cambridge Workshop material. It concluded with "The War in Heaven," which was performed by the ensemble without music.

Recreating the material through their own experiences proved to be an important learning process for the student actors. Working with character that was not linked to narrative, or with language that was seemingly characterless, as in parts of "Tongues," and using music and rhythm as an approach to character, helped expand the base of the performers' traditional technique. Although we ended up exploding "Tongues," we felt the restructuring was within the spirit of the creators. Our guide had been Shepard's statement in the notes to "Tongues": "The choices we made in performance were very personal and almost impossible to repeat on paper. These notes are only an indication of how we arrived at a means of collaboration. Anyone wishing to perform this piece would necessarily have to come to their own means and experiment according to their given situation."

—Barry Daniels
New York
May, 1994

Note: The Chaikin/Shepard recording of "The War in Heaven" is available on a cassette, *Joseph Chaikin Performs*, released by Raven Recordings in 1990.